G000123125

AI
11

AMERICAN ILLUSTRATION 11

EDITOR:
Edward Booth-Clibborn

PUBLISHER:
Kenneth Fadner

DESIGNER:
Gary Koepke

PRODUCTION MANAGER:
Laurence King

ART CONSULTANT:
Sebastian Buffa

PRODUCTION CO-ORDINATOR:
Mark Heflin, Jay Heflin

The artwork and the caption information in this book have been supplied by the entrants. While every effort has been made to ensure accuracy, American Illustration does not under any circumstances accept any responsibility for errors or omissions.

If you are a practicing illustrator, artist, or student, and would like to submit work to the next annual competition, write to: American Illustration, 49 East 21st Street, New York, NY 10010; (212) 979-4500.

Distributor to the U.S.A. Trade: Rizzoli International Publications, 300 Park Avenue South, New York, NY 10010-3599.

Distributed in the United Kingdom and World Direct Mail: Internos Books, 18 Colville Road, London W3 8BL U.K.

Distributor in France: Sofedis, 29 Rue Saint-Sulpice, Paris 75006 France.

Book trade for the rest of the world: Hearst Books International, 105 Madison Avenue, New York, NY 10016.

Copyright ©1992 Amilus, Inc.

Printed by Dai Nippon.

All rights reserved.

No part of this publication may be reproduced, stored in a retrieval system, or transmitted in any from or by any means — electronic, mechanical, photocopying, recording, or otherwise — without prior permission of the copyright owner.

CONTENTS

INTRODUCTION

For over ten years now I have worked with successive juries to select the very best paintings and drawings from the many thousands created each year by artists and illustrators working for North America's mass communications media.

In our time we have seen ideas and images which have appalled us, uplifted us, disgusted and inspired us.

We have been delighted, horrified and – at times – just plain bored.

But we have never lost sight of our original objective: to seek out the best work being done each year, and give it the space it deserves in "American Illustration."

This year our task was made more enjoyable by the very welcome submissions we had from students. The work of these young people has a vibrant and stimulating energy which, in some cases, easily makes up for any short-comings they may have in technique. And, of course, their view of the world is utterly their own, untrammeled by any of the compromises which sometimes stunt the more cautious illustrator's professional growth.

We also received many submissions from established illustrators working at the height of their powers. People like Marshall Arisman are featured again this year.

For me, this is the great strength of "American Illustration."

On the one hand, we can select and publish the work of unknown young people whose careers are just beginning. On the other, we are constantly being asked to pass judgement on work by people whose reputations are secure; people who, to a greater or lesser extent, have no need to submit anything to "American Illustration," other than the desire to be seen among their peers year in and year out.

With submissions running at much the same level as last year, my jury had the usual daunting task.

Yet, with their experience and talent for spotting talent, I knew they had the credentials for the challenge they faced.

Wendy Bass, for example, teaches at New York's School for Visual Arts, has worked in several publishing houses as a designer, and has won numerous awards from the Societies of Illustrators in New York and Los Angeles, the Bookbinders Guild of New York and the New York Art Directors Club.

Teresa Fernandes started work as an advertising art director in Canada. Since then she has worked on "Sports Illustrated," "Forum," "Travel Holiday," "Allure," "Arrow," "Toronto Life" and many other magazines. She is currently designing "The Savage Mirror," a book on the art of contemporary caricature. She has won many awards from professional organizations such as The Art Directors Club of Toronto, The Society of Publication Designers, The Society of Newspaper Designers and the Graphic Designers Association of Canada.

Gary Koepke is a gold and silver award winner at both The New York Art Directors Club, and the Society of Publication Designers. Since setting up his own business in 1987, he has designed a wide range of publications, including "Global Magazine" for Bull HN Information Systems, "26" for Agfa Corporation, "Colors" for Benetton, "World Tour" for Dun & Bradstreet Software and "Volume Magazine," a new music publication founded by Quincy Jones which is published by Time Publishing Ventures Inc..

Philippe Lardy is our illustrator. Co-editor of GIN and COMIX magazines with fellow illustrator Jose Ortega, Philippe's clients include "The New York Times," Bloomingdale's, "The Village Voice," United Airlines, AT&T and many other corporations. His work has won awards from The Society of Newspaper Designers and been featured in "American Illustration," "European Illustration" and "Communication Arts."

Founder of Studio W, Fo Wilson has had fifteen years experience as a designer and art director in publishing, and has won numerous awards for her work on magazines such as "Glamour," "Essence," "Sportswear International," "Savvy," "Woman's Day" and "The New York Times Magazine." She has taught at The School of Visual Arts and presently serves as an adjunct assistant professor at NYU's Centre for Publishing and as an instructor at Parsons School of Design.

Their good humored dedication to the job at hand made the selection of "American Illustration 11" much easier than it might have been. I thank them for their hard work, their insights and their vision.

Next year we shall have a new jury. There will be new work for us to enjoy, and I hope that, if you feel you want to, you will submit your work along with the many other artists and illustrators who, like me, want to show America and the rest of the world just how good American illustration is these days.

EDWARD BOOTH-CLIBBORN

IF BOTTICELLI

WERE ALIVE

TODAY HE'D

—PETER USTINOV

BE WORKING

FOR VOGUE

JOHN COLLIER

ART DIRECTOR: FRED WOODWARD
EDITOR: ANTHONY DE CURTIS   WRITER: MIKAL GILMORE
PUBLICATION: ROLLING STONE   DATE: JANUARY 24, 1991
PUBLISHING COMPANY: STRAIGHT ARROW PUBLISHERS
MEDIUM: PASTEL

"THE WONDER OF SINATRA," A RECORD REVIEW, WAS ACCOMPANIED BY THIS ILLUSTRATION.

JOHN COLLIER

ART DIRECTOR: FRED WOODWARD
EDITOR: BOB WALLACE   WRITER: NORMAN MAILER
PUBLICATION: ROLLING STONE
PUBLISHING COMPANY: STRAIGHT ARROW PUBLISHERS
MEDIUM: PASTEL
THIS ILLUSTRATION WAS CREATED FOR A BOOK EXCERPT ENTITLED "HARLOT'S GHOST."

11

CHRISTIAN CLAYTON

ART DIRECTOR: RICHARD LEEDS

EDITOR: DOMINIC MILANO   WRITER: ROBERT L. DOERSCHUK

PUBLICATION: KEYBOARD MAGAZINE   DATE: APRIL 1992   PUBLISHING COMPANY: MILLER FREEMAN PUBLICATIONS

MEDIUM: MIXED MEDIA

THE CONTINUING SAGA OF MARIAN MCPARTLAND'S AWARD-WINNING RADIO SHOW IS PORTRAYED IN THIS IMAGE.

GARY PANTER

DESIGN DIRECTOR: MICHAEL GROSSMAN   ART DIRECTOR: MARK MICHAELSON   DESIGNER: GREGORY MASTRIANNI

EDITOR: JAMES W. SEYMORE   WRITER: KEN TUCKER

PUBLICATION: ENTERTAINMENT WEEKLY   DATE: NOVEMBER 15, 1991

PUBLISHING COMPANY: THE TIME INC. MAGAZINE COMPANY

MEDIUM: INK ON ACETATE AND ACRYLIC ON PAPER

A BOOK REVIEW OF GREIL MARCUS' "DEAD ELVIS" FEATURED THIS ILLUSTRATION.

JOSH GOSFIELD

DESIGNER: CRAIG YOE

"THE ART OF MICKEY MOUSE" PORTRAYED NEW LOOKS OF THE OLD CHARACTER.

14

ERIC WHITE

ART DIRECTOR: BART NAGEL

EDITOR: R.U. SIRIUS   WRITER: BARBARA LEARY

PUBLICATION: MONDO 2000   DATE: JUNE 1991   PUBLISHING COMPANY: FUN CITY MEGAMEDIA

MEDIUM: ACRYLIC ON BOARD

"ANDY WARHOL'S SECRET DESIRE TO REJOIN HIS IDOL, WALT DISNEY" GAVE RISE TO THIS INTERPRETATION.

VIVIENNE FLESHER

ART DIRECTOR: CATHY NENNEKER

PUBLICATION: SHAPE MAGAZINE   **DATE: JUNE 1991**   **PUBLISHING COMPANY: WEIDER PUBLICATIONS**

MEDIUM: PASTEL ON PAPER

THESE TWO IMAGES APPEARED WITH AN ARTICLE ENTITLED "HEALTHY FOODS."

SCOTT MENCHIN

ART DIRECTOR: RHONDA RUBINSTEIN
EDITOR: TERRY McDONNELL   WRITER: JOHN UPDIKE
PUBLICATION: ESQUIRE   DATE: JUNE 1991   PUBLISHING COMPANY: HEARST CORPORATION
MEDIUM: INK AND WATERCOLOR
THESE FOUR IMAGES ACCOMPANIED AN ESQUIRE FEATURE CALLED "THE RUMOR."

TERESA BERASI

ART DIRECTOR: KENN NADEL

EDITOR: REBECCA GREER   WRITER: CONSTANCE STAPLETON

PUBLICATION: WOMAN'S DAY   DATE: MARCH 10, 1992   PUBLISHING COMPANY: HACHETTE MAGAZINES, INC.

MEDIUM: GOUACHE AND COLORED PENCIL

PRESERVING FAMILY HEIRLOOMS WAS THE SUBJECT OF THIS CUBISTIC STILL-LIFE FOR THE ARTICLE ENTITLED
"MAKING YOUR TREASURE LAST FOREVER."

TIM LEWIS

ART DIRECTOR: KENT HUNTER

EDITOR: DANNY ABELSON   WRITER: DANNY ABELSON

PUBLICATION: CULTURE AND CORPORATIONS   DATE: WINTER 1991   PUBLISHING COMPANY: SIMPSON PAPER COMPANY

MEDIUM: WATERCOLOR

SHOWING THE POSITIVE AND NEGATIVE SIDES OF THE ENVIRONMENT,

SIMPSON PAPER COMPANY DEMONSTRATES THE IMPORTANCE OF USING RECYCLED PAPER IN AN ARTICLE TITLED

"CULTURE AND PERCEPTION."

THOM SEVALRUD

ART DIRECTOR: JENNIFER HINRICHS
EDITOR: PATRISHA ROBERTSON   WRITER: JOANNE MACRAE
PUBLICATION: HEALTHWATCH MAGAZINE   DATE: NOVEMBER 1991   PUBLISHING COMPANY: TELEMEDIA PROCOM INC.
MEDIUM: WATERCOLOR, ACRYLIC AND PRISMACOLOR

THIS ILLUSTRATION ASKS THE QUESTION: ARE WE THROWING AWAY THE KEY THAT LINKS US
TO THE WORLD – OUR HEARING? FOR THE ARTICLE "ON THE EDGE OF SILENCE."

PHILIPPE WEISBECKER

ART DIRECTOR: RHONDA RUBINSTEIN
PUBLICATION: ESQUIRE MAGAZINE   MEDIUM: MIXED MEDIA
THIS COMMISSIONED YET UNPUBLISHED PIECE FOR ESQUIRE IS ENTITLED "LATIN AMERICAN STORY."

PHILIPPE WEISBECKER

ART DIRECTOR: GORDON SMITH   DESIGNER: CHARLENE CHARLES
EDITOR: THOMAS BROM   WRITER: CYNTHIA COOPER
PUBLICATION: CALIFORNIA LAWYER MAGAZINE   DATE: MAY 1991
MEDIUM: PEN, INK AND WATERCOLOR

THE SPECIALIZATION OF LAW SCHOOLS WAS THE SUBJECT OF THE ARTICLE FEATURING THIS ILLUSTRATION.

PHILIPPE WEISBECKER

ART DIRECTOR: PIERRE SERIES

PUBLICATION: FRENCH DAILY NEWSPAPER   DATE: JULY 1991   PUBLISHING COMPANY: LIBERATION

MEDIUM: GRAPHITE ON BROWN PAPER

THIS PIECE ACCOMPANIED A BOOK REVIEW OF "KGB LITERARY SECRET FILES."

PHILIPPE WEISBECKER

ART DIRECTOR: MIRKO ILIC   WRITER: JOELLE ATTINGER

PUBLICATION: TIME MAGAZINE INTERNATIONAL EDITION   DATE: JULY 5, 1991   PUBLISHING COMPANY: THE TIME INC. MAGAZINE COMPANY

MEDIUM: PENCIL AND BALL POINT PEN

THIS ILLUSTRATION, FOR THE ARTICLE "SAVOIR-VIVRE," DEPICTS VARIOUS ASPECTS OF HIGH CULTURE IN FRANCE.

PHILIPPE WEISBECKER

ART DIRECTOR: MARK BELLY

PUBLICATION: FRENCH DAILY NEWSPAPER   DATE: JUNE 1991   PUBLISHING COMPANY: LIBERATION

MEDIUM: PENCIL ON PAPER

A BOOK REVIEW OF RICHARD BRAUTIGAN'S "ROAD TO ABORTION" FEATURED THIS IMAGE.

BRIAN CRONIN

DESIGNER: KANDY LITTRELL   ART DIRECTOR: JANET FROELICH

EDITOR: WARREN HOGE   WRITER: ROGER ROSENBLATT

PUBLICATION: THE NEW YORK TIMES MAGAZINE   DATE: JANUARY 19, 1992

PUBLISHING COMPANY: NEW YORK TIMES COMPANY

MEDIUM: PEN, INK AND WATERCOLOR

THIS IMAGE REFLECTS THE POINTS MADE BY THE AUTHOR IN THE ESSAY "HOW TO END THE ABORTION WAR."

26

BRIAN CRONIN

ART DIRECTOR: JANET FROELICH

EDITOR: WARREN HOGE   WRITER: STEPHEN BUDIANSKY

PUBLICATION: THE NEW YORK TIMES MAGAZINE   DATE: DECEMBER 22, 1991

PUBLISHING COMPANY: NEW YORK TIMES COMPANY

MEDIUM: PEN, INK AND WATERCOLOR

THE ARTIST WAS ASKED TO INTERPRET THE ISSUE OF ANIMAL DOMESTICATION FOR THE ESSAY "IN FROM THE COLD."

BRIAN CRONIN

ART DIRECTOR: LUCY BARTHOLOMAY
EDITOR: ANDE ZELLMAN
PUBLICATION: THE BOSTON GLOBE MAGAZINE   DATE: APRIL 7, 1991
INDIVIDUAL LIBERTIES AND THE RIGHTS OF SOCIETY WERE THE SUBJECTS OF THE ARTICLE "A CONSTANT TEST OF FREEDOM."

BRIAN CRONIN

ART DIRECTOR: LUCY BARTHOLOMAY
EDITOR: ANDE ZELLMAN
PUBLICATION: THE BOSTON GLOBE MAGAZINE   DATE: APRIL 7, 1991
THE BOSTON GLOBE MAGAZINE RAN THIS ILLUSTRATION AS ITS COVER CELEBRATING 200 YEARS OF THE BILL OF RIGHTS.

BRIAN CRONIN

ART DIRECTOR: RICHARD BAKER

EDITOR: BOB THOMPSON   WRITER: MICHAEL NORMAN

PUBLICATION: THE WASHINGTON POST MAGAZINE   DATE: FEBRUARY 17, 1991

PUBLISHING COMPANY: WASHINGTON POST PUBLISHING COMPANY

MEDIUM: INK AND WATERCOLOR

THIS ILLUSTRATION APPEARED ALONGSIDE THE ARTICLE ''PEACE AND WAR.''

TOM WOODRUFF

ART DIRECTOR: FRED WOODWARD

EDITOR: ANTHONY DE CURTIS   WRITER: DAVID FRICKE

PUBLICATION: ROLLING STONE   DATE: JANUARY 23, 1992

PUBLISHING COMPANY: STRAIGHT ARROW PUBLISHERS

MEDIUM: OIL

THIS IMAGE APPEARED WITH THE REVIEW OF LOU REED'S "MAGIC & LOSS."

31

GARY KELLEY

ART DIRECTOR: JANE PALECEK

EDITOR: KARIN EVANS   EDITOR-IN-CHIEF: ERIC SCHRIER   WRITER: KUMIKO MAKIHARA

PUBLICATION: HEALTH   DATE: MAY–JUNE 1991   PUBLISHING COMPANY: HIPPOCRATES PARTNERS

MEDIUM: PASTEL ON PAPER

"DEATH OF A SALARYMAN" WAS THE TITLE OF THE ARTICLE FEATURING THESE THREE IMAGES.

GARY KELLEY

ART DIRECTOR: FRED WOODWARD
EDITOR: PETER TRAVERS   WRITER: PETER TRAVERS
PUBLICATION: ROLLING STONE   DATE: MAY 30, 1991   PUBLISHING COMPANY: STRAIGHT ARROW PUBLISHERS
MEDIUM: PASTEL
"MADONNA CAUSES A COMMOTION," A REVIEW OF "TRUTH OR DARE," FEATURED THIS ILLUSTRATION.

BILLY MALONE

ART DIRECTOR: JENNIFER JESSEE
PUBLICATION: CAMPUS VOICE   DATE:
PUBLISHING COMPANY: WHITTLE COMMUNICATIONS
MEDIUM: 3-D
THIS 3-D IMAGE APPEARED IN THE MARCH 1991 ISSUE OF THE MAGAZINE CAMPUS VOICE.

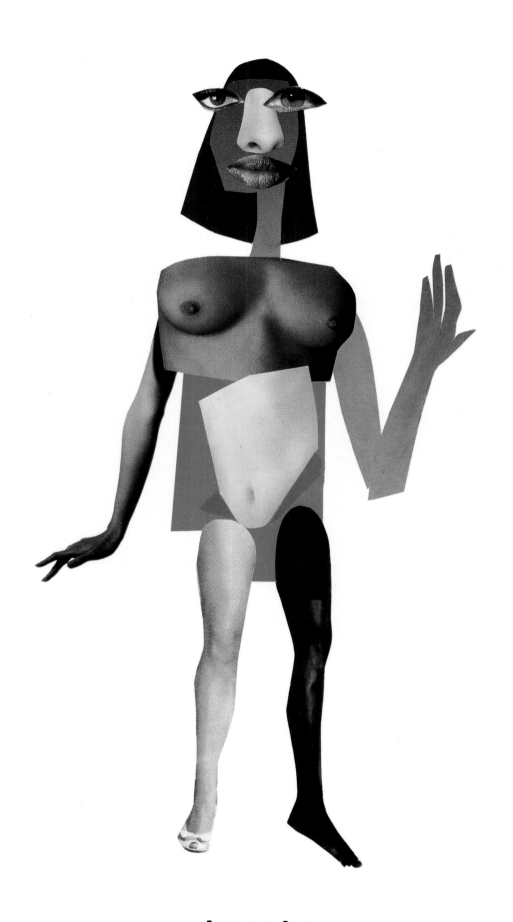

ABIRA ALI

DESIGNER: LEIGH BRADFORD   ART DIRECTOR: JOEL BERG
EDITOR: AMY GROSS   WRITER: AMY PAGNOZZI
PUBLICATION: MIRABELLA MAGAZINE   DATE: SEPTEMBER 1991
PUBLISHING COMPANY: MURDOCK MAGAZINES
MEDIUM: COLLAGE
INCREASING INTERRACIAL MARRIAGE WAS THE TOPIC FOR THE ARTICLE "MIXING IT UP."

FILIP PAGOWSKI

ART DIRECTOR: FRANCESCA RESTREPO
PUBLICATION: I LOVE NEW YORK – I HATE NEW YORK. NEW MUSIC SEMINAR CASSETTE
DATE: JULY 1991   PUBLISHING COMPANY: SONY MUSIC, COLUMBIA RECORDS
MEDIUM: INK ON PAPER

THIS MAP WAS PROVIDED FOR OUT OF TOWN MUSIC INDUSTRY EXECUTIVES COMING FOR THE ANNUAL NEW MUSIC SEMINAR EVENT.

RICHARD DOWNS

DESIGNER: KATHY MARTY   ART DIRECTOR: JANE PALECEK

EDITOR: ERIC W. SCHRIER, SHERIDAN WARRICK   WRITER: PETER JARET

PUBLICATION: HEALTH   DATE: MARCH–APRIL 1991   PUBLISHING COMPANY: HIPPOCRATES PARTNERS

MEDIUM: ETCHING

THE FACT THAT MARATHON RUNNERS OFTEN DEVELOP COLDS AFTER A RACE IS REPRESENTED IN THIS ILLUSTRATION,

FOR "THE COLD TRUTHS ABOUT HARD WORKOUTS."

STEPHEN KRONINGER

DESIGN DIRECTOR: MICHAEL GROSSMAN   DESIGNER: GREGORY MASTRIANNI   ART DIRECTOR: MARK MICHAELSON
EDITOR: JAMES W. SEYMORE   WRITER: ARMOND WHITE
PUBLICATION: ENTERTAINMENT WEEKLY   DATE: SEPTEMBER 27, 1991   PUBLISHING COMPANY: THE TIME INC. MAGAZINE COMPANY
MEDIUM: CUT PAPER AND IMAGES IN COLLAGE
THIS ILLUSTRATION DEMONSTRATES HOW PUBLIC ENEMY PUTS THE NEWS OF THE DAY
ON THE DANCE FLOOR. FOR THE ARTICLE "'APOCALYPSE' NOW."

STEPHEN KRONINGER

DESIGN DIRECTOR: INA SALTZ   ART DIRECTOR: RUDOLPH C. HOGLUND

WRITER: LEON JAROFF

PUBLICATION: TIME MAGAZINE   DATE: AUGUST 26, 1991

PUBLISHING COMPANY: THE TIME INC. MAGAZINE COMPANY

MEDIUM: PAPER COLLAGE

A CRAZED SCIENTIST REFLECTS THE "CRISIS IN THE LABS" – BESET BY LOW BUDGETS, FRAUD, ACTIVISTS AND SKEPTICS.

WARREN LINN

ART DIRECTOR: NANCY SMITH

EDITOR: ROBIN MORGAN   WRITER: PATRICIA WILLIAMS

PUBLICATION: MS. MAGAZINE   PUBLISHING COMPANY: LANG COMMUNICATIONS

MEDIUM: COLLAGE AND SCRATCHBOARD

THIS IMAGE OF A WOMAN REMOVING HER GAG ILLUSTRATED THE ARTICLE "REFUSING TO BE SILENCED."

BLAIR DRAWSON

ART DIRECTOR: DONNA CRIVELLO

EDITOR: ELIZABETH LARGE   WRITER: JILL MORROW

PUBLICATION: THE BALTIMORE SUN   DATE: AUGUST 11, 1991

MEDIUM: ACRYLIC ON PAPER

"TOYING WITH FATE" WAS THE TITLE OF THE ARTICLE FEATURING THIS ILLUSTRATION.

PHILIP BURKE

ART DIRECTOR: CHARLES CHURCHWARD
EDITOR: TINA BROWN   WRITER: NORMAN MAILER
PUBLICATION: VANITY FAIR   DATE: MAY 1991   PUBLISHING COMPANY: CONDÉ NAST PUBLICATIONS, INC.
MEDIUM: OIL ON CANVAS
THIS PORTRAIT OF PRESIDENT GEORGE BUSH ACCOMPANIED THE ARTICLE "HOW THE WIMP WON THE WAR."

PHILIP BURKE

ART DIRECTOR: CHARLES CHURCHWARD

EDITOR: TINA BROWN   WRITER: NORMAN MAILER

PUBLICATION: VANITY FAIR   DATE: MARCH 1991   PUBLISHING COMPANY: CONDÉ NAST PUBLICATIONS, INC.

MEDIUM: OIL ON CANVAS

PORTRAIT OF BRET EASTON ELLIS, AUTHOR OF "AMERICAN PSYCHO," FOR AN ARTICLE ENTITLED "CHILDREN OF THE PIED PIPER."

HENRIK DRESCHER

DESIGN DIRECTOR: MICHAEL GROSSMAN   DESIGNER: ELIZABETH BETTS
EDITOR: JAMES W. SEYMORE   WRITER: OWEN GLEIBERMAN
PUBLICATION: ENTERTAINMENT WEEKLY   DATE: DECEMBER 27, 1991
PUBLISHING COMPANY: THE TIME INC. MAGAZINE COMPANY   MEDIUM: MIXED MEDIA

ENTERTAINMENT WEEKLY FEATURED THIS IMAGE WHEN IT NAMED "SILENCE OF THE LAMBS" MOVIE OF THE YEAR FOR 1991.

PAMELA HOBBS

ART DIRECTOR: BART NAGEL
DATE: JUNE 18, 1991
PUBLISHING COMPANY: MONDO 2000
MEDIUM: COMPUTER GRAPHICS AND ALDUS FREEHAND 3.1
THIS ILLUSTRATION IS ENTITLED "SMART DRUGS."

PATRICK BLACKWELL

ART DIRECTOR: LINDA J. KOURY
PUBLICATION: GBH, THE MEMBER'S MAGAZINE   DATE: APRIL 1991
PUBLISHING COMPANY: MARBLEHEAD COMMUNICATIONS
MEDIUM: INDIA INK AND PANTONE OVERLAY
"AMERICA'S SCHOOLS: WHO GIVES A DAMN?"
A TELEVISION DISCUSSION WHICH EXAMINED OUR EDUCATION SYSTEM.

STEVEN GUARNACCIA

DESIGNER: KANDY LITTRELL   ART DIRECTOR: JANET FROELICH

EDITOR: ROBERT VARE   WRITER: DAVID OSBORNE

PUBLICATION: THE NEW YORK TIMES MAGAZINE   DATE: MARCH 1, 1992

PUBLISHING COMPANY: NEW YORK TIMES COMPANY

MEDIUM: MARKER, COLORED PENCIL AND PACKING PAPER

A "GOVERNMENT THAT MEANS BUSINESS" INSPIRED THIS ILLUSTRATION OF THE MAD SCIENTIST.

STEFANO VITALE

DESIGNER: FO WILSON   ART DIRECTOR: DIANA LA GUARDIA
PUBLICATION: CONDÉ NAST TRAVELER   DATE: SPRING 1991
PUBLISHING COMPANY: CONDÉ NAST PUBLICATIONS, INC.
MEDIUM: OIL ON WOOD
MAN'S PLACE IN NATURE IS THE SUBJECT OF THIS ILLUSTRATION, FOR THE ARTICLE "MAN IN NATURE."
50

STEFANO VITALE

ART DIRECTOR: MARK ULRIKSEN
PUBLICATION: SAN FRANCISCO FOCUS   DATE: JANUARY 1991
MEDIUM: OIL ON WOOD

CONDITIONS IN HAITI WERE THE SUBJECT OF THIS ARTICLE,
"HAITI: A TRIP THROUGH HEAVEN AND HELL ON EARTH."

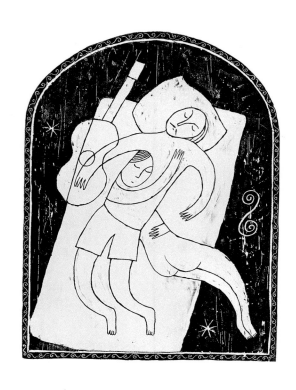

STEFANO VITALE

ART DIRECTOR: PAMELA BERRY   WRITER: ISABEL ALLENDE

PUBLICATION: SAVVY WOMAN   DATE: FEBRUARY 1991

PUBLISHING COMPANY: FAMILY MEDIA

MEDIUM: WOODCUT

THE STORY "THE WICKED GIRL" WAS ACCOMPANIED BY THIS ILLUSTRATION.

NORMAND COUSINEAU

ART DIRECTOR: ANDREE LAUZON
WRITER: JACQUES LANGUIRAND
PUBLICATION: GUIDE RESSOURCES   DATE: OCTOBER 1991
MEDIUM: GOUACHE, INK, CRAYONS AND BLEACH
THE NECESSITY OF HELP FROM OTHERS IN ORDER TO OVERCOME AN INFERIORITY COMPLEX
IS EXEMPLIFIED IN THIS ILLUSTRATION.

PHILIPPE LARDY

ART DIRECTOR: JACKIE SEGAL
PUBLICATION: NEWSDAY MAGAZINE   PUBLISHING COMPANY: TIMES - MIRROR
MEDIUM: GOUACHE
THIS ILLUSTRATION WAS USED AS THE COVER FOR NEWSDAY MAGAZINE CELEBRATING THE COMING OF SPRING.

GWYN STRAMLER

ART DIRECTOR: TINA ADAMEK

WRITER: JOEL K. KAHN M.D.   PUBLICATION: POSTGRADUATE MEDICINE

DATE: MAY 1, 1991   PUBLISHING COMPANY: MCGRAW-HILL INC.

MEDIUM: WATERCOLOR AND ACRYLIC

COPING WITH PHYSICAL DEBILITATION BROUGHT ON BY PROGRESSIVE HEART FAILURE
IS REVEALED IN THIS IMAGE FOR THE ARTICLE "CONGESTIVE HEART FAILURE."

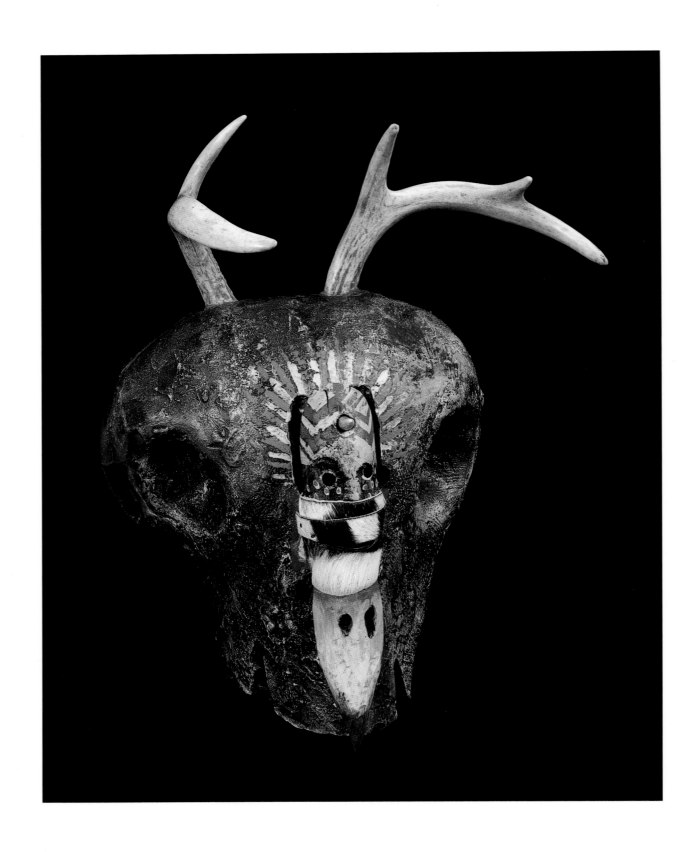

MARSHALL ARISMAN

ART DIRECTOR: JANET FROELICH

EDITOR: WARREN HOGE   WRITER: STEPHEN BUDIANSKY

PUBLICATION: THE NEW YORK TIMES MAGAZINE   DATE: DECEMBER 22, 1991

PUBLISHING COMPANY: NEW YORK TIMES COMPANY

ANIMAL DOMESTICATION IS THE SUBJECT AND INSPIRATION FOR THIS IMAGE.

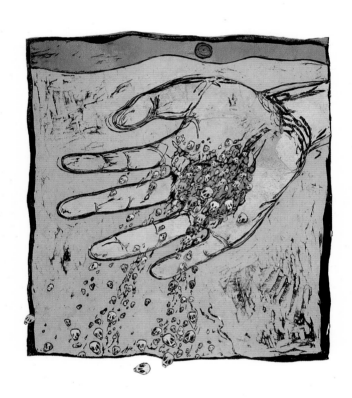

FRANCES JETTER

DESIGN DIRECTOR: INA SALTZ   ART DIRECTOR: RUDOLPH C. HOGLUND

WRITER: LANCE MORROW   PUBLICATION: TIME MAGAZINE   DATE: APRIL 1, 1991

PUBLISHING COMPANY: THE TIME INC. MAGAZINE COMPANY

MEDIUM: LINOLEUM CUT

A REFLECTION ON THE PERSIAN GULF WAR WAS THE SUBJECT FOR "A MOMENT FOR THE DEAD."

ALAN E. COBER

ART DIRECTOR: RONALD F. ARNHOLM
EDITOR: STANLEY LINDBERG   WRITER: RICHARD N. JOHNSON
PUBLICATION: THE GEORGIA REVIEW   DATE: FALL 1991
PUBLISHING COMPANY: THE UNIVERSITY OF GEORGIA
MEDIUM: WATERCOLOR
"PIG'S HEAD, CAPE COD."

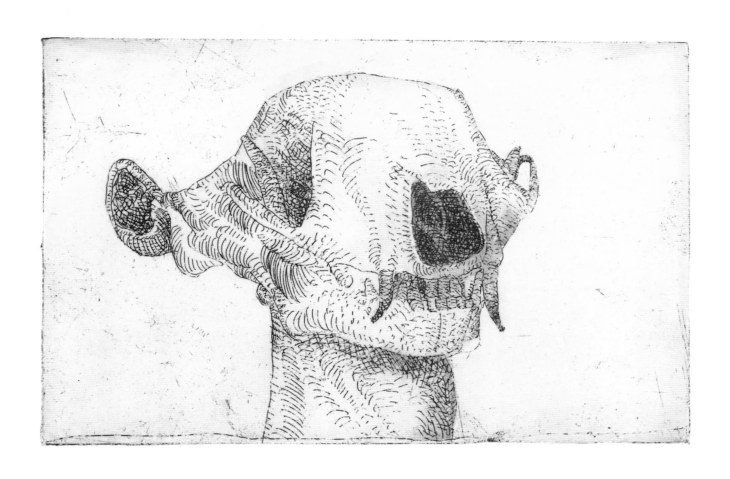

ALAN E. COBER

ART DIRECTOR: RONALD F. ARNHOLM
EDITOR: STANLEY W. LINDBERG   WRITER: RICHARD N. JOHNSON
PUBLICATION: THE GEORGIA REVIEW   DATE: FALL 1991
PUBLISHING COMPANY: THE UNIVERSITY OF GEORGIA
MEDIUM: ETCHING

"SKUNK MAN."

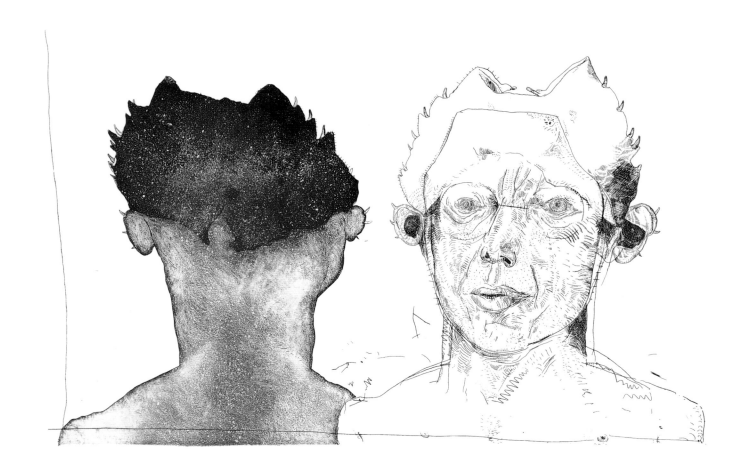

ALAN E. COBER

ART DIRECTOR: RONALD F. ARNHOLM
EDITOR: STANLEY LINDBERG   WRITER: RICHARD N. JOHNSON
PUBLICATION: THE GEORGIA REVIEW   DATE: FALL 1991   PUBLISHING COMPANY: THE UNIVERSITY OF GEORGIA
MEDIUM: ETCHING WITH AQUATINT
"SELF-PORTRAIT, FRONT AND BACK, WITH HELMET,"
FROM AN ARTICLE ON "ALAN E. COBER: BEHIND THE LINES."

ALAN E. COBER

ART DIRECTOR: RONALD F. ARNHOLM
EDITOR: STANLEY LINDBERG   WRITER: RICHARD N. JOHNSON
PUBLICATION: THE GEORGIA REVIEW   DATE: FALL 1991
PUBLISHING COMPANY: UNIVERSITY OF GEORGIA
MEDIUM: ETCHING WITH AQUATINT
THIS ETCHING IS TITLED "CONVERSATION FOR ONE,"
FROM THE SAME ARTICLE.

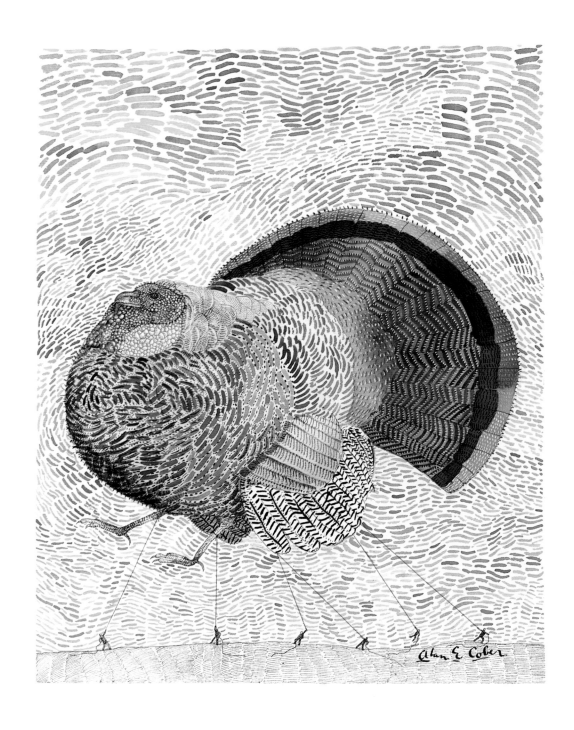

ALAN E. COBER

ART DIRECTOR: RENA SOKOLOW
PUBLICATION: THE BOSTON GLOBE   DATE: NOVEMBER 28, 1991
MEDIUM: INK AND WATERCOLOR
THIS TURKEY WAS FEATURED ON THE COVER OF THE BOSTON GLOBE'S THANKSGIVING DAY "CALENDAR" SECTION.

ALAN E. COBER

ART DIRECTOR: LUCY BARTHOLOMAY
EDITOR: ANDE ZELLMAN   WRITER: DAVID ROBERTS
PUBLICATION: THE BOSTON GLOBE   DATE: JANUARY 13, 1991
MEDIUM: INK AND WATERCOLOR
THIS ILLUSTRATION WAS INCLUDED WITH THE ARTICLE "THE REAL AMADEUS,"
WHICH ATTEMPTED TO DISPROVE THE IMAGE OF MOZART AS A BUFFOON.

LAURA LEVINE

DESIGNER: GARY KOEPKE   ART DIRECTOR: TIBOR KALMAN
WRITER: TIBOR KALMAN AND KARRIE JACOBS
PUBLICATION: COLORS   DATE: SPRING–SUMMER 1992   PUBLISHING COMPANY: BENETTON GROUP S.P.A.
MEDIUM: ACRYLIC ON MASONITE BOARD

SHOWING SEVERAL HAIRSTYLES FROM AROUND THE WORLD,
THIS ILLUSTRATION APPEARED WITH AN ARTICLE ENTITLED "HAIR."

JULIE DELTON

ART DIRECTOR: TIM BROWN

EDITOR: LEONARD WITT   WRITER: TIMOTHY BRADY

PUBLICATION: MINNESOTA MONTHLY   DATE: SEPTEMBER 1991

PUBLISHING COMPANY: MINNESOTA MONTHLY, ON BEHALF OF MINNESOTA PUBLIC RADIO

MEDIUM: WATERCOLOR AND INK

"IT COULD BE VERSE," AN ARTICLE ON PERFORMING POETS INCLUDED THIS ILLUSTRATION.

LILLA ROGERS

ART DIRECTOR: DON MORRIS   WRITER: DYLAN LANDIS
PUBLICATION: METROPOLITAN HOME   DATE: FEBRUARY 1992
MEDIUM: OIL ON LINEN
THESE TWO PIECES ILLUSTRATED THE ARTICLE "WHAT DESIGNERS KNOW: THE POWER OF PAINT."

GERALD BUSTAMANTE

ART DIRECTORS: JEFF DARNALL, DAVID CARSON

EDITOR: LINDA LEWIN

PUBLICATION: ECO MAGAZINE   DATE: JANUARY 1992

PUBLISHING COMPANY: MICHAEL FELDMAN

MEDIUM: ACRYLIC ON PAPER

THIS ILLUSTRATION FOR ECO MAGAZINE IS TITLED "LOVE AND THE WATER CYCLE."

JOHN HERSEY

ART DIRECTOR: JOANNE HOFFMAN   WRITER: DAVID POGUE
PUBLICATION: MACWORLD
PUBLISHING COMPANY: MACWORLD COMMUNICATIONS
MEDIUM: MACINTOSH COMPUTER
THIS IMAGE ILLUSTRATES THE EASE OF USING MACROS FOR "THE DESK POTATO'S GUIDE TO MACROS."

ROY PENDLETON

ART DIRECTOR: LEN WILLIS   WRITER: DAVID MORRELL
PUBLICATION: PLAYBOY   DATE: FEBRUARY 1991
MEDIUM: TRANSPARENT ACRYLICS
ACTOR SYLVESTER STALLONE'S CHARACTER WAS DISCUSSED IN THE ARTICLE "THE MAN WHO CREATED RAMBO."

JANET WOOLLEY

ART DIRECTOR: CAROL LAYTON

EDITOR: CURTIS HARTMAN   WRITER: DEIRDRE FANNING

PUBLICATION: WORTH   DATE: FEBRUARY–MARCH 1992

PUBLISHING COMPANY: CAPITAL PUBLISHING

MEDIUM: MIXED MEDIA

"THE PRINCE CHARLES SYNDROME: WAITING FOR THE DOUGH" WAS THE TITLE OF THE ARTICLE WHICH FEATURED THIS IMAGE.

BARRY BLITT

ART DIRECTOR: FRED WOODWARD   EDITOR: ANTHONY DE CURTIS
WRITER: ROBERT PALMER
PUBLICATION: ROLLING STONE   DATE: MAY 16, 1991
PUBLISHING COMPANY: STRAIGHT ARROW PUBLISHERS
MEDIUM: PEN AND INK AND WATERCOLOR
THIS ILLUSTRATION ACCOMPANIED A RECORD REVIEW ENTITLED "DANGER HIGH VOLTAGE FROM STAX."

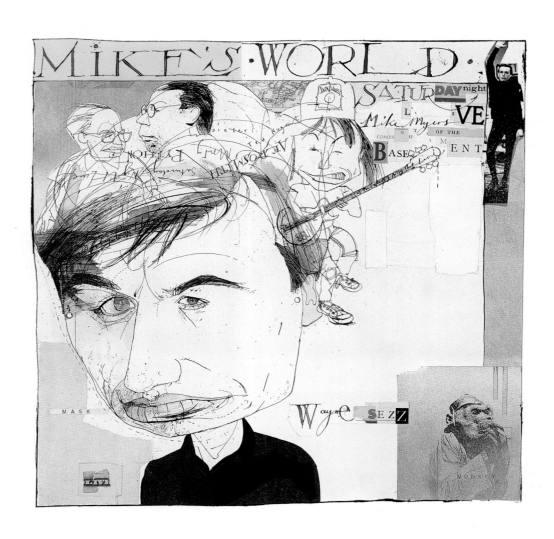

DAVID HUGHES

ART DIRECTOR: JENNIFER JESSEE   EDITOR: CAROLE SIMMONS
PUBLICATION: CAMPUS VOICE   PUBLISHING COMPANY: WHITTLE COMMUNICATIONS
MEDIUM: COLLAGE OF WATERCOLORS AND INK.
THIS ILLUSTRATION, ENTITLED "MIKE'S WORLD," RAN IN CAMPUS VOICE.

ROB DAY

ART DIRECTOR: SAROYAN HUMPHREY   EDITOR: TOM WHEELER   WRITER: JAS OBRECHT

PUBLICATION: GUITAR PLAYER   DATE: JULY 1991   PUBLISHING COMPANY: MILLER FREEMAN PUBLICATIONS

MEDIUM: OIL ON PAPER

AN ARTICLE IN GUITAR PLAYER INCLUDED THIS PORTRAIT OF LEGENDARY BLUES GUITARIST BLIND LEMON JEFFERSON.

ROB DAY

DESIGNER: BETH GOLDSTEIN   ART DIRECTOR: RICHARD BLEIWEISS   EDITOR: PETER BLOCH   WRITER: EMILY PRAGER
PUBLICATION: PENTHOUSE   DATE: SEPTEMBER 1991   PUBLISHING COMPANY: PENTHOUSE INTERNATIONAL, LTD.
MEDIUM: OIL ON PAPER

A STORY ENTITLED "THE RETURN OF COOL" ABOUT CONTEMPORARY POP STARS AND THE LACK OF CONTENT
IN THE IMAGES THEY PROJECT INCLUDED THIS PORTRAIT OF MADONNA.

PAULA MUNCK

ART DIRECTOR: TANYA ROBERSON   EDITOR: MARGARET MUCKLO
PUBLICATION: PINNACLE MAGAZINE   DATE: MAY 1991
PUBLISHING COMPANY: KELLY COMMUNICATIONS
MEDIUM: ACRYLIC AND GOUACHE
THIS ILLUSTRATION ACCOMPANIED A PIECE CALLED "CHECKPOINTS – STAGING YOUR CARNEGIE HALL DEBUT."

JUDY PEDERSEN

ART DIRECTOR: KEIKO HIRAYAMA

PUBLICATION: HANATSUBAKI   DATE: 1991   PUBLISHING COMPANY: SHISEIDO

MEDIUM: MIXED MEDIA

DANCE PIONEER MARTHA GRAHAM WAS HONORED IN HANATSUBAKI IN A REGULAR FEATURE CALLED PORTRAITS.

C. F. PAYNE

DESIGNER: DOROTHY MARSCHALL   ART DIRECTOR: JANE PALECEK
EDITOR: SHERIDAN WARRICK   EDITOR-IN-CHIEF: ERIC SCHRIER   WRITER: PATRICIA LONG
PUBLICATION: HEALTH   DATE: FEBRUARY-MARCH 1992
PUBLISHING COMPANY: HIPPOCRATES PARTNERS
MEDIUM: MIXED MEDIA - OIL, ACRYLIC, WATERCOLOR, PENCILS
AN ARTICLE ENTITLED "THE GREAT WEIGHT DEBATE" FEATURED THIS IMAGE.

BRAD HOLLAND

ART DIRECTOR: LAURA LUOSTRARINEN

THIS ILLUSTRATION WAS USED AS A POSTER FOR THE MIKKELI ART MUSEUM IN FINLAND.

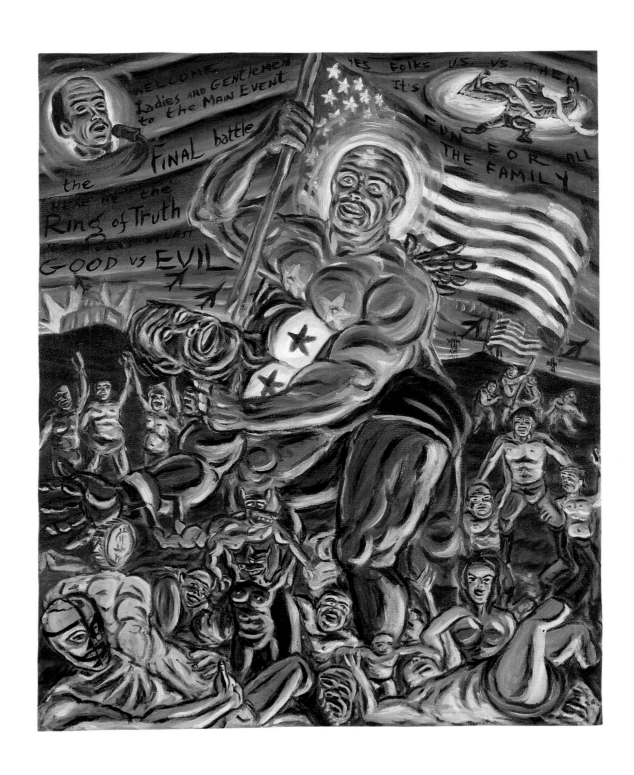

DAVID SANDLIN

DESIGN DIRECTOR: MICHAEL GROSSMAN   ART DIRECTOR: ROBERT NEWMAN   DESIGNER: ELIZABETH BETTS

EDITOR: JAMES W. SEYMORE   WRITER: TY BURR

PUBLICATION: ENTERTAINMENT WEEKLY   DATE: MAY 3, 1991   PUBLISHING COMPANY: THE TIME INC. MAGAZINE COMPANY

MEDIUM: OIL ON CANVAS

THIS ILLUSTRATION, FOR THE ARTICLE "STRANGE BRUTES," REPRESENTS HOW WRESTLEMANIA VII

WON THE CHAMPIONSHIP OF TRASH ENTERTAINMENT.

CHARLES BURNS

DESIGNER: KANDY LITTRELL   ART DIRECTOR: JANET FROELICH
EDITOR: WARREN HOGE   WRITER: KEN AULETTA
PUBLICATION: THE NEW YORK TIMES MAGAZINE   DATE: JULY 28, 1991
PUBLISHING COMPANY: NEW YORK TIMES COMPANY
MEDIUM: WATERCOLOR AND GUACHE
THIS ILLUSTRATION, PORTRAYING A DAZED ABC AFTER SURVIVING THE BATTLE OF THE TV NETWORKS,
WAS USED ON THE MAGAZINE'S COVER FOR THE STORY "WHY ABC SURVIVED BEST."

PIERRE FORTIN

ART DIRECTOR: JACQUELINE MOORBY

EDITOR: JERRY TUTUNJIAN   WRITER: DAVID MENZIES

PUBLICATION: CANADIAN HOTELS AND RESTAURANTS   PUBLISHING COMPANY: MACLEAN HUNTER LTD.

MEDIUM: INK

THE MISERY AND GRIEF OF THE DRINKING AND DRIVING VICTIM WAS EXPLORED IN THIS ILLUSTRATION,
APPEARING ALONGSIDE THE ARTICLE "JUST SAY NO!"

ROBERT NEUBECKER

ART DIRECTOR: DAVID HERBICK   WRITER: JONATHAN ALTER
PUBLICATION: NEWSWEEK   DATE: OCTOBER 14, 1991
PUBLISHING COMPANY: THE WASHINGTON POST COMPANY
MEDIUM: WATERCOLOR, INK AND PASTEL
THIS ILLUSTRATION DEMONSTRATES HOW POLITICIANS MANIPULATE THE MEDIA,
FOR THE ARTICLE "NO BULL. THE CAMPAIGN AMERICA NEEDS."

PETER KUPER

ART DIRECTOR: ALEX HA   WRITER: JONATHAN ALTER

PUBLICATION: NEWSWEEK   DATE: OCTOBER 28, 1991

PUBLISHING COMPANY: THE WASHINGTON POST COMPANY

MEDIUM: STENCIL, ENAMEL, PAINT AND COLLAGE

"THE MEDIA EAT THEIR OWN-THE THOMAS EFFECT" INSPIRED THIS ILLUSTRATION.

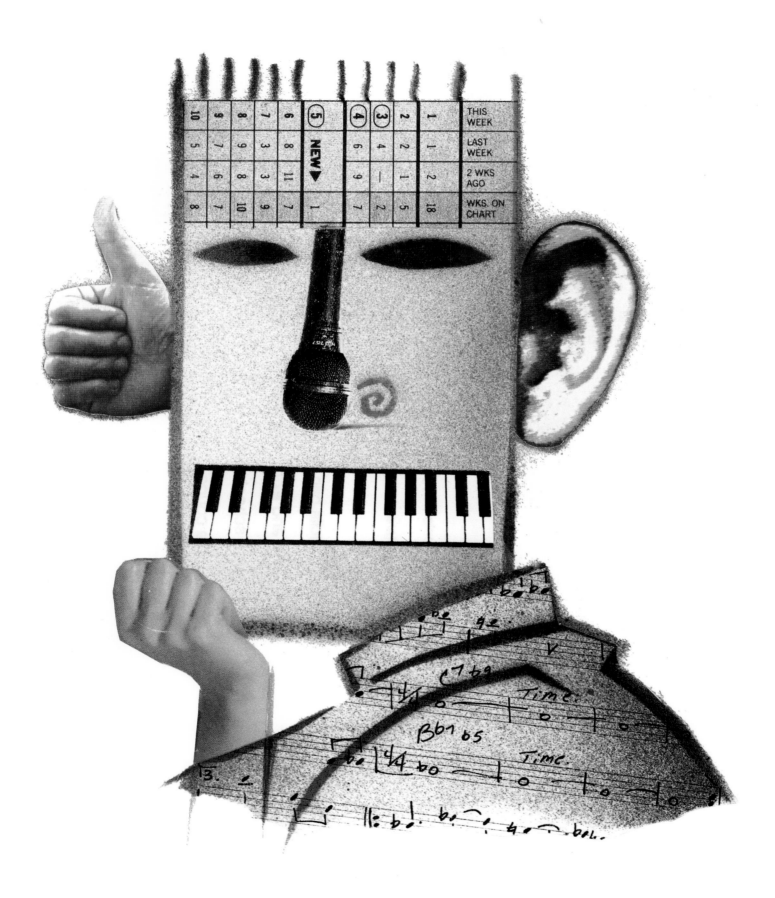

PETER KUPER

ART DIRECTOR: CHARLENE BENSON   WRITER: STEPHEN FRIED
PUBLICATION: GENTLEMEN'S QUARTERLY   DATE: JANUARY 1992
PUBLISHING COMPANY: CONDÉ NAST PUBLICATIONS INC.
THIS IMAGE ILLUSTRATED GQ'S REVIEW "SOUND BITES: THE BEST OF 1991."

PETER KUPER

ART DIRECTOR: RICHARD BAKER, KELLY DOE   EDITOR: BOB THOMPSON
WRITER: HOWARD KURTZ
PUBLICATION: THE WASHINGTON POST MAGAZINE   DATE: SEPTEMBER 22, 1991
PUBLISHING COMPANY: WASHINGTON POST PUBLISHING COMPANY
MEDIUM: STENCIL, ENAMEL PAINT WITH WATERCOLOR, COLORED PENCIL AND COLLAGE
THE ARTICLE "THE POLITICS OF SCANDALS" FEATURED THIS ILLUSTRATION.

MELISSA GRIMES

ART DIRECTOR: KERRY TREMAIN
EDITOR: DOUG FOSTER   WRITER: BEN H. BAGDIKIAN
PUBLICATION: MOTHER JONES MAGAZINE   DATE: MAY–JUNE 1992
PUBLISHING COMPANY: FOUNDATION FOR NATIONAL PROGRESS
MEDIUM: COLLAGE

"JOURNALISM OF JOY" IS THE TITLE OF THE ARTICLE WHICH FEATURED THIS COLLAGE.

EDWARD SOREL

ART DIRECTOR: JUDY GARLAN

EDITOR: WILLIAM WHITWORTH   WRITER: NANCY CALDWELL SOREL

PUBLICATION: THE ATLANTIC MONTHLY   DATE: NOVEMBER 1991

MEDIUM: PASTEL ON COLORED PAPER

THIS ILLUSTRATION OF CHURCHILL AND STALIN DISCUSSING WHERE THE "SECOND FRONT" SHOULD TAKE PLACE
APPEARED WITH THE ARTICLE "FIRST ENCOUNTERS."

STEVE CARVER

ART DIRECTOR: ALEX ISLEY   EDITOR: DUNCAN CHRISTY   WRITER: GEOFFREY NORMAN
PUBLICATION: FORBES FYI   DATE: OCTOBER–NOVEMBER 1991   PUBLISHING COMPANY: FORBES INC.
MEDIUM: ACRYLIC–ALKYD
EX-GENERAL SCHWARTZKOPF – AT EASE – FOR "AT EASE WITH THE GENERAL."

89

JOHN KASCHT

ART DIRECTOR: CLAIRE INNES
PUBLICATION: THE DETROIT FREE PRESS   DATE: SEPTEMBER 23, 1991
MEDIUM: WATERCOLOR AND DYES
"HALSTON: THE HEIGHT OF PASSION" INCLUDED THIS CARICATURE OF THE DESIGNER.

MALCOLM TARLOFSKY

ART DIRECTOR: DAVID ARMARIO   EDITOR: MARC ZABLUDOFF   WRITER: ROBERT SAPOLSKY

PUBLICATION: DISCOVER MAGAZINE   DATE: MARCH 1992   PUBLISHING COMPANY: DISNEY MAGAZINES

MEDIUM: PHOTO-COLLAGE

NEUROPSYCHIATRIC ODDITIES AND OTHER ABNORMAL BEHAVIOR ARE DISCUSSED IN THIS ARTICLE, "HOW BIG IS YOURS?"

GARY BASEMAN

ART DIRECTOR: ALEXA MULVIHILL   WRITER: WENDY TAYLOR

PUBLICATION: PC COMPUTING   DATE: FEBRUARY 1992

MEDIUM: MIXED MEDIA

THE SUBJECT OF COMPUTER VIRUSES WAS DISCUSSED IN AN ARTICLE FEATURING THIS IMAGE.

LANE SMITH

ART DIRECTOR: JESSICA HELFAND
EDITOR: FRED MANN   WRITER: LINDA K. HARRIS
PUBLICATION: PHILADELPHIA INQUIRER   DATE: OCTOBER 20, 1991
MEDIUM: MIXED MEDIA
AN ARTICLE ENTITLED "DOING THE WRITE THING" FEATURED THIS IMAGE.

JOHN BACKDERF

MEDIUM: PEN AND INK

THIS SYNDICATED COMIC STRIP APPEARED IN SEVERAL NEWSPAPERS AROUND THE COUNTRY.

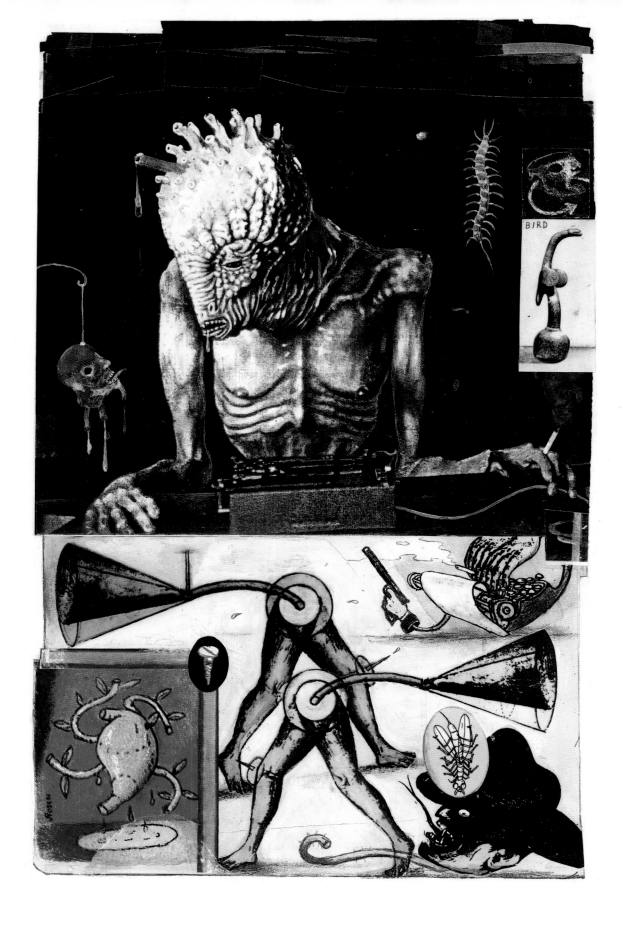

JONATHON ROSEN

ART DIRECTOR: FRED WOODWARD
PUBLICATION: ROLLING STONE   DATE: FEBRUARY 6, 1992
PUBLISHING COMPANY: STRAIGHT ARROW PUBLISHING INC.
MEDIUM: ACRYLIC, WATERCOLOR AND COPIER TONER ON PAPER. MOUNTED ON BOARD.
A SYMBOLIC INTERPRETATION OF DAVID CRONENBERG'S MOVIE
ADAPTATION OF WILLIAM BURROUGH'S NOVEL "NAKED LUNCH."

AMY GUIP

DESIGNER: JUDY GARLAN   ART DIRECTOR: ROBIN GILMORE-BARNES
WRITER: FRANCIS DAVIS
PUBLICATION: THE ATLANTIC MONTHLY   DATE: APRIL 1991
MEDIUM: MIXED MEDIA
THIS ILLUSTRATION ACCOMPANIED "BLUES WALKING LIKE A MAN," A MUSIC REVIEW OF ROBERT JOHNSON.

AMY GUIP

DESIGN DIRECTOR: MICHAEL GROSSMAN   DESIGNER: ELIZABETH BETTS
EDITOR: JAMES W. SEYMORE   WRITER: OWEN GLEIBERMAN
PUBLICATION: ENTERTAINMENT WEEKLY   DATE: JULY 5, 1991   PUBLISHING COMPANY: THE TIME INC. MAGAZINE COMPANY
MEDIUM: COLLAGE
MOVIES ARE POP DREAMS, AND SUMMER IS THE DREAM SEASON. FROM THE ARTICLE "APPLAUSE AND EFFECTS."

SANDRA DIONISI

DESIGNER: JUDY GARLAN
EDITOR: WILLIAM WHITWORTH   WRITER: ROBBIE CLIPPER SETHI
PUBLICATION: THE ATLANTIC MONTHLY MAGAZINE   DATE: AUGUST 1991
MEDIUM: GOUACHE
A FICTIONAL PORTRAIT OF THE MAIN CHARACTER IN THE ARTICLE "GRACE,"
DEPICTING AN AMERICAN WOMAN WHO MARRIES INTO AN EAST INDIAN FAMILY.

SANDRA DIONISI

ART DIRECTOR: GAIL ANDERSON   WRITER: SPENCER HARRINGTON
PUBLICATION: ROLLING STONE MAGAZINE   DATE: OCTOBER 31, 1991
PUBLISHING COMPANY: STRAIGHT ARROW PUBLISHERS INC.
MEDIUM: GOUACHE
"TRAGIC BLUES" – A PORTRAIT OF BILLIE HOLIDAY FOR THE ARTICLE
"THE LIGHT & DAY OF LADY DAY."

CURTIS PARKER

ART DIRECTOR: PETER HATCHER   EDITOR: JEFF BERGER
PUBLICATION: BECHTEL BRIEFS   DATE: JULY 1991
PUBLISHING COMPANY: BECHTEL CORPORATION
MEDIUM: DR. MARTIN'S WATERCOLOR ON ILLUSTRATION BOARD
BECHTEL CORPORATION'S EFFORTS IN DEVELOPING NEW WAYS TO CUT EMISSIONS
WAS THE INSPIRATION FOR THIS ILLUSTRATION.

BENOIT

ART DIRECTOR: LEE LORENZ
PUBLICATION: THE NEW YORKER   DATE: JUNE 24, 1991
MEDIUM: OIL ON PAPER
THIS ILLUSTRATION WAS USED ON THE COVER OF THE NEW YORKER.

MARIS BISHOFS

ART DIRECTOR: MIRKO ILIC   WRITER: PETER SCHNEIDER
PUBLICATION: TIME MAGAZINE INTERNATIONAL EDITION   DATE: JULY 1, 1991
PUBLISHING COMPANY: THE TIME INC. MAGAZINE COMPANY
MEDIUM: ACRYLIC

THE PROBLEM OF EAST AND WEST GERMAN RE-UNIFICATION IS THE TOPIC OF THIS ESSAY, "BELATED MARRIAGE."

MARIS BISHOFS

ART DIRECTOR: RUDOLPH C. HOGLUND   DESIGN DIRECTOR: INA SALTZ
WRITER: MICHAEL KINSLEY
PUBLICATION: TIME MAGAZINE   DATE: MAY 13, 1991
PUBLISHING COMPANY: THE TIME INC. MAGAZINE COMPANY
MEDIUM: ACRYLIC
THIS IMAGE PORTRAYED THE TOPIC IN THE ESSAY "PLEASE DON'T QUOTE ME."

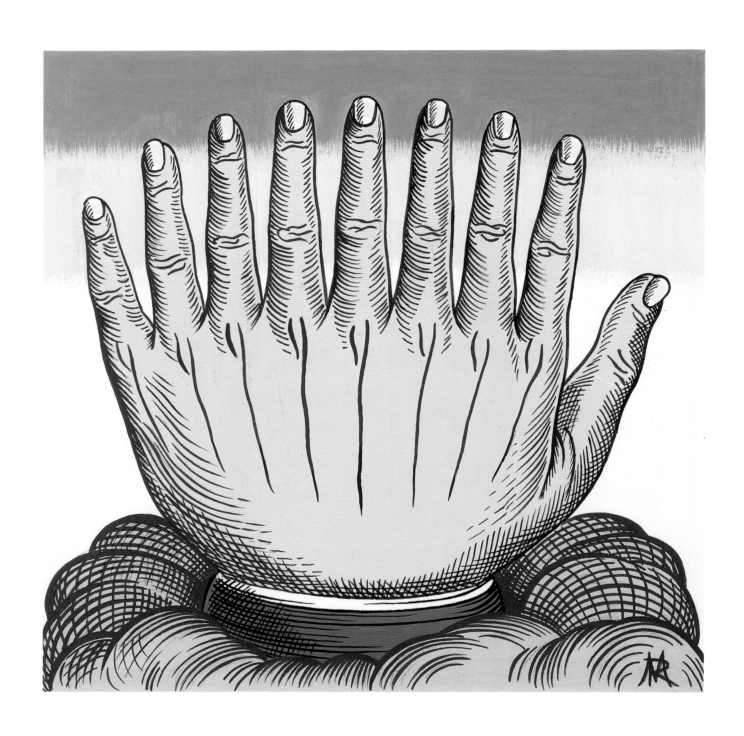

RUTH MARTEN

DESIGN DIRECTOR: INA SALTZ   ART DIRECTOR: RUDOLPH C. HOGLUND
WRITER: PICO IYER
PUBLICATION: TIME MAGAZINE   DATE: SEPTEMBER 16, 1991
PUBLISHING COMPANY: THE TIME INC. MAGAZINE COMPANY
MEDIUM: GOUACHE
THIS IMAGE REFLECTS THE ESSAY'S TOPIC: THE MAGIC OF THE NUMBER 9.

JULIAN ALLEN

ART DIRECTOR: EDWARD BOOTH-CLIBBORN
PUBLICATION: AMERICAN ILLUSTRATION 10
MEDIUM: WATERCOLOR AND COLLAGE
''THE FOUNDERS OF AMERICAN ILLUSTRATION.''

JORDIN ISIP

ART DIRECTOR: PATRICK J.B. FLYNN   EDITOR: ERWIN KROLL   WRITER: MANNING MARABLE
PUBLICATION: THE PROGRESSIVE   DATE: NOVEMBER 1991
PUBLISHING COMPANY: THE PROGRESSIVE, INC.
MEDIUM: CHARCOAL, GESSO AND NEWSPAPER
THIS ILLUSTRATION ACCOMPANIED THE ARTICLE "BLACK AMERICA IN SEARCH OF ITSELF."

JORDIN ISIP

ART DIRECTOR: NOEL CLARO   EDITOR: MARY KAYE SCHILLING   WRITER: KIM FRANCE

PUBLICATION: SASSY   DATE: APRIL 1992

PUBLISHING COMPANY: LANG COMMUNICATIONS

MEDIUM: MIXED MEDIA

THE ARTICLE "ARE YOU A CYNIC?" FEATURED THIS IMAGE.

A MIGHTY

BOOKS

BLOODLESS

SUBSTITUTE

—ROBERT LOUIS STEVENSON

FOR LIFE

JONATHON ROSEN

ART DIRECTOR: NICKERBOCKER   WRITER: JONATHON ROSEN

MAGAZINE TITLE: NOZONE   DATE PUBLISHED: 1991

MEDIUM: COPIER TONAL SEPARATION FROM A MIXED MEDIA DRAWING

SCIENTIST ACTING AS GOD AND CONTROLLING THE BIOLOGICAL DESTINY OF THE HUMAN SPECIES AND LIFE ON EARTH.

JONATHON ROSEN

EDITOR: GLEN HEAD, KAZ
DATE PUBLISHED: MARCH 1992   PUBLISHING COMPANY: FANTAGRAPHICS BOOKS
MEDIUM: ACRYLIC, WATERCOLOR, AND COPIER TONER ON PAPER
THIS IMAGE WAS USED AS THE COVER OF "SNAKE EYES," THE SELF EXPLORATION PUBLICATION.

REGENERATION

Pat Barker

ROBERT CLYDE ANDERSON

ART DIRECTOR: MICHAEL IAN KAYE   EDITOR: WILLIAM ABRAHAMS   WRITER: PAT BARKER

DATE PUBLISHED: FALL 1991   PUBLISHING COMPANY: DUTTON

MEDIUM: GOUACHE

USED AS THE COVER, "REGENERATION"

EXPLORES THE TIMELESS PSYCHOLOGICAL PROBLEMS MILITARY MEN ENCOUNTER IN A POST WAR SOCIETY.

TERRY ALLEN

ART DIRECTORS: CRAIG YOE, JANET MORRA-YOE
PUBLISHING COMPANY: HYPERION BOOKS
MEDIUM: GOUACHE
"THE ART OF MICKEY MOUSE" INCLUDED THIS IMAGE ENTITLED "MEESE'S PIECES."

LANE SMITH

ART DIRECTOR: MOLLY LEACH   EDITOR: REGINA HAYES
PUBLISHING COMPANY: VIKING PENGUIN
MEDIUM: OIL

THIS SERIES OF FOUR IMAGES ILLUSTRATED A CHILDREN'S BOOK
ENTITLED "GLASSES, WHO NEEDS 'EM?"

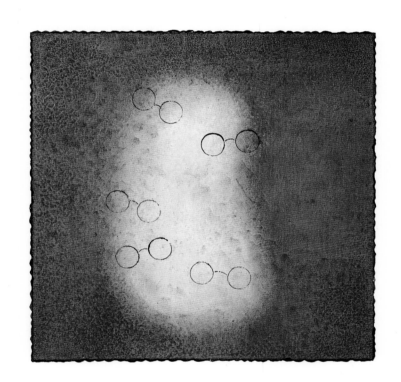

L A N E S M I T H

LANE SMITH

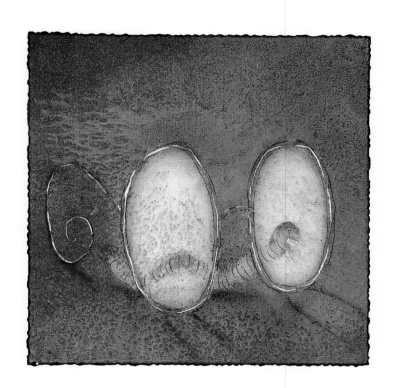

LANE SMITH

SALLY MARA STURMAN

ART DIRECTOR: SUSAN MITCHELL   EDITOR: LUANN WALTHER   WRITER: WILLA CATHER

BOOK TITLE: COLLECTED STORIES OF WILLA CATHER   DATE PUBLISHED: APRIL 1991

PUBLISHING COMPANY: VINTAGE BOOKS

MEDIUM: OIL CRAYON

THIS ILLUSTRATION ACCOMPANIED "WAGNER'S MATINEE" IN A COLLECTION OF SHORT STORIES.

BRAD HOLLAND

ART DIRECTOR: TOM EGNER
DATE: MAY 1992
PUBLISHING COMPANY: AVON BOOKS
MEDIUM: ACRYLIC
THIS IMAGE APPEARED IN THE PUBLICATION "THE BACHELORS."

NORMAND COUSINEAU

ART DIRECTOR: GARY BEELIK   PUBLISHING COMPANY: HBJ HOLT – CANADA

BOOK TITLE: PERSPECTIVES 3   DATE PUBLISHED: SEPTEMBER 1992

MEDIUM: GOUACHE AND INK

CHAPTER OPENER OF A TEXTBOOK FOR ADOLESCENTS ENTITLED "WHEN ARE YOU GOING TO GROW UP?"

NORMAND COUSINEAU

ART DIRECTOR: GIANNI CACCIA   EDITOR: ANTONIO D'ALFONSO   WRITER: NADINE LTAIF
BOOK TITLE: ENTRE LES FLEURES   DATE PUBLISHED: SEPTEMBER 1991
PUBLISHING COMPANY: GUERNICA
MEDIUM: GOUACHE, EGG YOLK, OIL, PASTEL
ILLUSTRATION FOR A POETRY BOOK WRITTEN BY A WOMAN WHOSE HEART IS TORN BETWEEN TWO COUNTRIES.

NANCY STAHL

ART DIRECTOR: WENDY BASS   EDITOR: SUZANNE KIRK   WRITER: SIMON BRETT
PUBLISHING COMPANY: SCRIBNERS
MEDIUM: GOUACHE
THE MYSTERY NOVEL "CORPORATE BODIES" FEATURED THIS ILLUSTRATION AS ITS COVER.

OWEN SMITH

ART DIRECTOR: SUSAN MITCHELL   WRITER: THOMAS SANCHEZ

PUBLISHING COMPANY: VINTAGE CONTEMPORARIES

MEDIUM: OIL ON BOARD

THIS PAINTING WAS FEATURED AS THE COVER OF "ZOOT-SUIT MURDERS," A MYSTERY SET IN THE 1940'S.

BRIAN CRONIN

ART DIRECTOR: CAROL DEVINE CARSON   WRITER: JOAN FRANCES CASEY

DATE PUBLISHED: JULY 1991   PUBLISHING COMPANY: ALFRED A. KNOPF INC.

MEDIUM: PEN, INK AND WATERCOLOR

"THE FLOCK," AN AUTOBIOGRAPHICAL ACCOUNT

OF A MULTIPLE PERSONALITY FEATURED THIS IMAGE AS ITS COVER.

MARK RYDEN

ART DIRECTOR: CATHERINE VANDECASTEELE   WRITER: CAROLE KOENIG
BOOK TITLE: LA411, 13TH EDITION   DATE: JANUARY 1992
MEDIUM: ACRYLIC
THIS SERIES OF THREE ILLUSTRATIONS WAS USED AS THE COVER AND DIVIDER PAGES FOR THE
"PROFESSIONAL REFERENCE GUIDE TO FILM PRODUCTION." BEING THE 13TH EDITION, THE IMAGES EXAMINE SUPERSTITIONS.

MARK RYDEN

MARK RYDEN

A POLITE

EUPHEMISM

FOR

—WALTER LIPPMANN

DECEPTION

PAULA MUNCK

ART DIRECTOR: PAUL COURNOYER   WRITER: MICHELE MCKENNA   AGENCY: COLE & WEBER
MEDIUM: ACRYLIC AND GOUACHE
THESE THREE IMAGES WERE PART OF A CAMPAIGN FOR WESTIN HOTELS AND RESORTS.

P A U L A   M U N C K

PAULA MUNCK

ANTHONY RUSSO

MEDIUM: ACRYLICS
THIS IMAGE IS ENTITLED "BODY PARTS."

JOSE ORTEGA

ART DIRECTORS: LIVIA DAZA PARIS, CARLOS TARACHE
MEDIUM: FIVE COLOR SILKSCREEN
THIS ILLUSTRATION WAS USED ON A T-SHIRT FOR CAONABÓ,
A FESTIVAL OF NEW DANCE FORMS IN THE AMERICAS HELD IN CARACAS.

JOSE ORTEGA

ART DIRECTOR: FREDERIQUE CORCIA
MEDIUM: SCRATCHBOARD AND WATERCOLORS
ONE IN A SERIES OF FIVE CD COVERS FOR GITANES JAZZ IN BRAZIL.

137

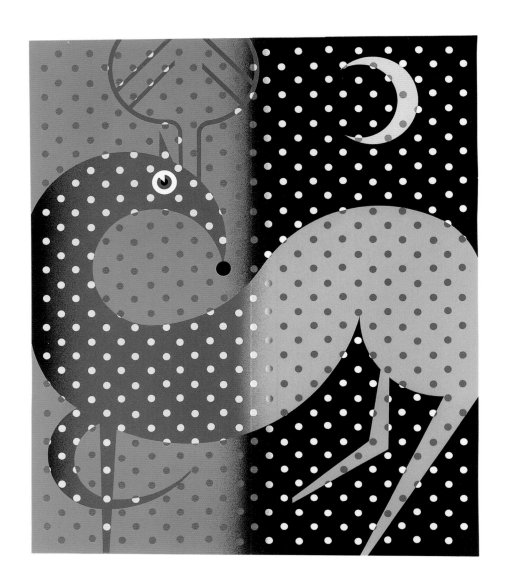

TERRY ALLEN

ART DIRECTOR: EDDIE NUNNS

MEDIUM: GOUACHE

THIS REINDEER WAS USED FOR THE NEIMAN-MARCUS 1991 CHRISTMAS BOOK.

GERALD BUSTAMANTE

ART DIRECTOR: SCOTT MIRES   EDITOR: DEBORAH LIV JOHNSON   WRITER: MICHAEL HILTON

DATE: MAY 1992   CLIENT: ADVENTURE 16 OUTDOOR AND TRAVEL OUTFITTERS

MEDIUM: CARVED BOARD, ACRYLIC AND ASSEMBLAGE

THIS ILLUSTRATION SUGGESTS THAT BEING IN THE WILDERNESS CAN PROVIDE INSIGHT INTO ONE'S OWN NATURE,

RELATIONSHIPS WITH OTHERS, AND THE WORLD IN WHICH WE LIVE.

PAMELA HOBBS

ART DIRECTOR: DON GATTERDAM
DATE: JANUARY 30, 1992
MEDIUM: COMPUTER GRAPHICS – PHOTOSHOP 2.0
"ABSOLUTE ALTERNATIVE." AN ADVERTISEMENT FOR ABSOLUTE VODKA.

JEFF FISHER

ART DIRECTOR: TIM GALLES

MEDIUM: ACRYLIC AND PAINT

A PROMOTIONAL PIECE FOR THE TIME INC. MAGAZINE COMPANY ENCOURAGING EDUCATION.

JEFF FISHER

ART DIRECTOR: SUSAN HOCHBAUM

CLIENT: CHAMPION COMPANY

MEDIUM: SEPARATED ARTWORK AND SCREENPRINT

THIS PORTRAYAL OF CATHERINE THE GREAT'S VANITY WAS USED AS A PROMOTION FOR CHAMPION PAPER COMPANY.

JEFF FISHER

ART DIRECTOR: SANDY KAUFMAN
MEDIUM: ACRYLIC AND PAINT

THIS POSTER WAS CREATED TO DEMONSTRATE THE ATTRACTIONS OF ACADEMIC LIFE AT NEW YORK UNIVERSITY.

IVAN CHERMAYEFF

EDITOR: WALTER SCHWAIGER
MEDIUM: COLLAGE AND MIXED MEDIA
"SOS KINDERDÖRFER: HELFEN WELTWEIT." THIS IS AN AGENCY HELPING CHILDREN WORLDWIDE.

DOUGLAS FRASER

ART DIRECTOR: PAUL ASAO

MEDIUM: ALKYDS AND COLOR COPIES ON PAPER

A FESTIVAL IN TAMPA CELEBRATING CONTEMPORARY VISUAL, PERFORMANCE AND MUSICAL ARTS INSPIRED THIS ILLUSTRATION.

MIKE BENNY

ART DIRECTOR: BOB BEYN
CLIENT: SERAPHEIN BEYN ADVERTISING
MEDIUM: ACRYLIC
THIS PORTRAIT OF HONUS WAGNER EXEMPLIFIES THE CLIENT'S HARD HITTING STYLE OF ADVERTISING.

MILTON GLASER

MEDIUM: COLORED PENCIL AND WATERCOLOR
THE WORK WAS COMMISIONED FOR THE METROPOLITAN OPERA TO PROMOTE THE 200TH ANNIVERSARY OF MOZART'S BIRTHDAY, "MOZART 200".

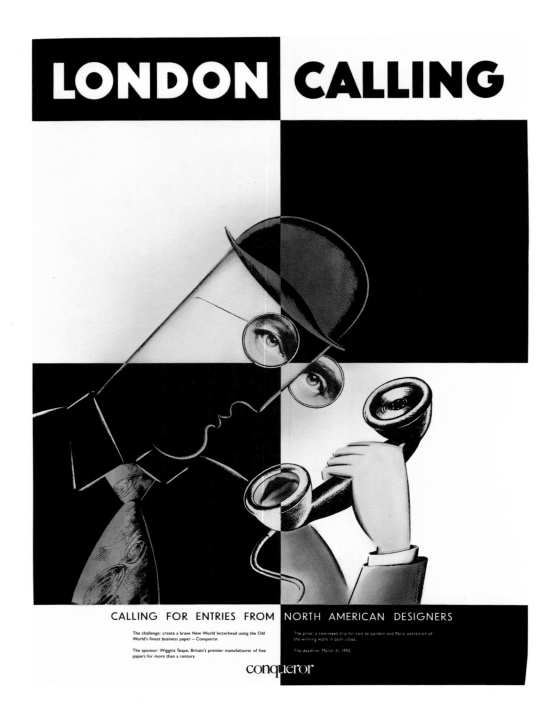

FRANK VIVA

WRITER: DOUG DOLAN

DATE: SEPTEMBER 1991

PUBLISHING COMPANY: ARJO WIGGINS

MEDIUM: CHALK AND WATERCOLOR

THIS POSTER PROMPTED ENTRIES TO A DESIGN COMPETITION FOR A BRITISH PAPER COMPANY.

FRANK VIVA

WRITER: DOUG DOLAN

MEDIUM: CHALK AND WATERCOLOR

THE EXCITEMENT OF THE OSCARS WAS CAPTURED IN THIS POSTER FOR A FILM FESTIVAL FUND-RAISER IN ONTARIO.

149

THE PERFECT

DESIGN

USE OF AN

—OSCAR WILDE

IMPERFECT

MEDIUM

C H R I S T I A N   C L A Y T O N

A RT D IRECTOR: R ICHARD D OWNS
M EDIUM: M IXED MEDIA
A PIECE CREATED FOR THE BAND M IGHTY J OE Y OUNG.

Ezekiel Gibbs

CHRISTIAN CLAYTON

MEDIUM: MIXED MEDIA

THIS IS ONE IN A SERIES OF PAINTINGS INSPIRED BY BLACK VISIONARIES.

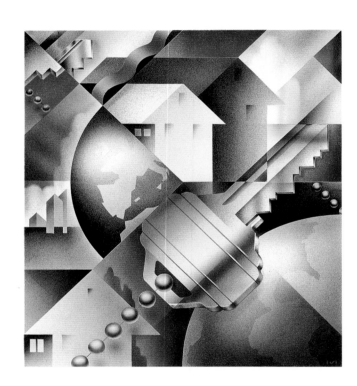

JOHN MATTOS

ART DIRECTOR: STEPHEN MARTIN

MEDIUM: INK ON PAPER

THE COVER OF KAUFMAN & BROAD'S 1991 ANNUAL REPORT FEATURED THIS ILLUSTRATION.

CHRISTIAN NORTHEAST

MEDIUM: MIXED MEDIA

A PERSONAL PROMOTIONAL PIECE EXPERIMENTING IN THE USE OF A COMIC FORMAT.

PHIL HULING

ART DIRECTORS: ELLEN CLANCY, GREG DOBOS
WRITER: MARCIA POLESE
MEDIUM: PENCIL AND INK OIL WASH
THESE ILLUSTRATIONS WERE USED ON A MUTUAL FUND INFORMATION BROCHURE.

BRIAN CRONIN

MEDIUM: PEN AND INK AND LETTER PRESS PRINTING
A SELF PROMOTIONAL PIECE.

PHILIPPE WEISBECKER

ART DIRECTOR: ALAIN LACHARTRE

DATE: WINTER 1991   CLIENT: CHANEL

MEDIUM: MIXED MEDIA

THIS ILLUSTRATION DEPICTS THE BATTLE BETWEEN INDIGO IMPORTERS AND PASTEL MANUFACTURERS IN 18TH CENTURY FRANCE.

PHILIPPE WEISBECKER

MEDIUM: PENCIL ON SHOPPING BAG
FROM VUE SUR LA VILLE'S 1992 PROMOTIONAL CALENDAR.

BETH ADAMS

MEDIUM: GOUACHE AND INK ON PAPER.

THIS ILLUSTRATION WAS USED AS A SCARF FOR A FALL 1992 COLLECTION.

GARY BASEMAN

A PERSONAL PIECE INSPIRED BY THE CONTROLLED MEDIA COVERAGE OF THE GULF WAR.

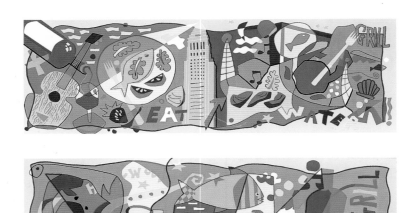

ANN FIELD

ART DIRECTOR: MARY OEFFLING

MEDIUM: ACRYLIC AND PAINT ON CANVAS. MOUNTED ON WOOD PANEL

A LOS ANGELES RESTAURANT USED THESE INTERIOR MURALS FOR PROMOTIONAL PURPOSES.

PHILIPPE LARDY

ART DIRECTOR: JIM CHRISTIE

THESE STYLIZED HUMAN FIGURES ARE FOUND ON BLOOMINGDALE'S SHOPPING BAGS CELEBRATING THE ARRIVAL OF 1992.

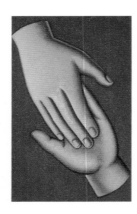

SANDRA DIONISI

ART DIRECTOR: SUNIL BHANDARI
WRITER: HELEN BATTERSBY
DATE: DECEMBER 1991   DESIGNER: HARRIS-BHANDARI DESIGN ASSOCIATES
MEDIUM: ACRYLIC ON PAPER
A DEPICTION OF THE SENSES ASSOCIATED WITH CHRISTMAS: SMELL (APPLE), FEEL (HANDS) AND TASTE (WINE).

JONATHON ROSEN

ART DIRECTOR: STEPHEN BYRAM
RECORD TITLE: 3 MERRY WIDOWS
MEDIUM: COPIER TONER, ACRYLIC MEDIUM AND WATERCOLOR ON PAPER. MOUNTED ON WOOD PANEL
A CD COVER COMBINING LATE MEDIEVAL ITALIAN FRESCO AND LATE 1960'S SAN FRANCISCO STYLES IN A SHOTGUN WEDDING.

KURT VARGO

WRITER: BRIAN GLEESON

DATE: MAY 1992

MEDIUM: PASTELS, INK AND COLLAGE

A PROMOTIONAL MAILER FOR RABBIT EARS INC.

FEATURED THIS ILLUSTRATION ANNOUNCING THE PREVIEW OF

"THE TIGER AND THE BRAHMIN" APPEARING ON SHOWTIME CABLE TV.

JORDIN ISIP

ART DIRECTOR: MELINDA BECK
COMPANY: WRECK AGE
MEDIUM: MIXED MEDIA
A RECORD COVER FOR BAD TRIP'S ALBUM "FEAR AND LOATHING."

BRIAN BARRINGTON

EDITOR: BRUCE ELLIOT

PUBLICATION TITLE: JOHN SIMON, PIECES OF THE FRAME   DATE: 1992   COMPANY: PLAIN WRAP PRODUCTIONS INC.

MEDIUM: SCRATCH BOARD, ACRYLIC AND OIL

CREATED FOR AN ALBUM COVER, THIS IMAGE ILLUSTRATES THE COMPLETE ORDER AND DISORDER OF OUR EMOTIONAL MAKE-UP AND REVEALS

THE UNSEEN FORCES OF LUST, OBSESSION, AND RAGE THAT AFFECT MORTAL BEHAVIOR.

JOEL NAKAMURA

DESIGNER: NANCY DONALD   ART DIRECTOR: DAVID COLEMAN
DATE: MARCH–APRIL   PUBLISHING COMPANY: SONY MUSIC
MEDIUM: MIXED MEDIA
"ALL OVER THE WORLD" IS THE TITLE OF THIS ILLUSTRATION CREATED FOR A CD LONG BOX.

ROSS MacDONALD

DESIGNER: CONCRETE DESIGN

MEDIUM: WATERCOLOR

THESE TWO IMAGES WERE USED ON A SELF-PROMOTIONAL CALENDAR.

ROSS MACDONALD

JOHN CRAIG

ART DIRECTOR: DAVID WILLETT
MEDIUM: COLLAGE AND OVERLAYS
THIS IMAGE ILLUSTRATES HOW TO BUILD THE PERFECT PEANUT.

MICHAEL BARTALOS

ART DIRECTOR: TATSUOMI MAJIMA

DATE: OCTOBER 1991   CLIENT: GULLIVER BOOK CO.

MEDIUM: CUT PAPER

THIS IMAGE IS ONE IN A SERIES OF PROMOTIONAL POSTCARDS.

IT'S EITHER

EASY OR

—SALVADOR DALI

IMPOSSIBLE

MARY LYNN BLASUTTA

MEDIUM: WATERCOLOR
A SELF PROMOTIONAL PIECE.

JESSIE HARTLAND

ART DIRECTOR: SUSUMU FUJII
EDITOR: YAMATO SHIINE   WRITER: MITSUKO KURODA
PUBLICATION TITLE: HANAKO MAGAZINE   DATE: MARCH 14, 1991
PUBLISHING COMPANY: MAGAZINE HOUSE LTD., TOKYO, JAPAN
MEDIUM: WATERCOLOR AND GOUACHE
THIS MAP WAS CREATED FOR THE HANAKO MAGAZINE ARTICLE "SAFARI IN KENYA."

JACK CLIGGETT

WRITER: LISA WALKER

PUBLICATION: PRINT MAGAZINE COMPUTER ART & DESIGN ANNUAL

PUBLISHING COMPANY: R.C. PUBLICATIONS INC.

MEDIUM: DIGITAL-PRINT MATCH

A COMBINATION OF FOUR DIFFERENT IMAGES,

THIS ILLUSTRATION EXPLORES THE MYTHOLOGICAL IMAGERY OF THE DESCENT TO THE UNDERWORLD.

BARBARA NESSIM

MEDIUM: COMPUTER DRAWING PAINTED WITH GOUACHE
"WHISPERS IN THE WIND."

BARBARA NESSIM

MEDIUM: COMPUTER DRAWING PAINTED WITH GOUACHE

"FAMILY DINNER."

ONE WHOSE

UNPUBLISHED

CAREER

—JAMES McNEILL WHISTLER

ALWAYS BEGINS

TOMORROW

ERIC DONELAN

MEDIUM: MIXED MEDIA

SELF-PROMOTIONAL PIECE FROM A SERIES ON EVERYDAY LIFE ENTITLED "TIRED OF WORK."

ERIC DONELAN

MEDIUM: MIXED MEDIA

SELF-PROMOTIONAL PIECE EXPLORING THE MANY HYPNOTIC ASPECTS OF MASS MEDIA.

TRAIAN ALEXANDRU FILIP

"LE MASSACRE DES INNOCENTS."

184

CLAYTON PREUITT

MEDIUM: ACRYLIC

A STUDY OF THE PHYSICAL CONSTRAINT AND ENCLOSURE OF SPACE UPON THE SUBJECT.

JESSICA FETTERER

MEDIUM: OIL ON CANVAS

FEBRUARY 1992

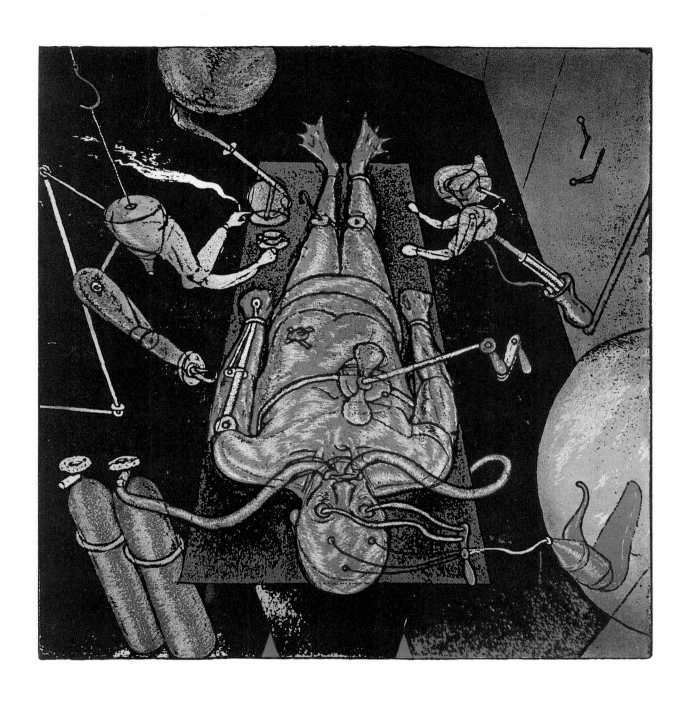

JONATHON ROSEN

MEDIUM: RELIEF ETCHING AND LINOLEUM PRINT ON PAPER
A LIMITED EDITION PRINT OF A MUTANT HUMANOID ON AN OPERATING TABLE.

CHRISTIAN NORTHEAST

MEDIUM: MIXED MEDIA
"HEALING COLOUR" TO BE PUBLISHED IN HEALTHWATCH MAGAZINE.

CHRISTIAN NORTHEAST

MEDIUM: MIXED MEDIA

THIS PERSONAL PIECE WAS USED FOR PROMOTIONAL PURPOSES.

CHRISTIAN NORTHEAST

MEDIUM: MIXED MEDIA

THIS PIECE WAS INSPIRED BY TIM O'BRIEN'S NOVEL "THE NUCLEAR AGE."

CHRISTIAN NORTHEAST

MEDIUM: MIXED MEDIA

THE CIRCUS-CARNIVAL QUALITY OF 19TH CENTURY TRADING CARDS WAS THE INSPIRATION FOR THIS ILLUSTRATION.

JOSE ORTEGA

ART DIRECTORS: FRAN BLACK, LONA BENNEY

MEDIUM: FOUR COLOR SILKSCREEN

A HALLOWEEN POSTER FOR THE ARTS COUNCIL, USED AS SELF-PROMOTION BY THE ARTIST.

HAYES HENDERSON

ART DIRECTOR: DAVID CARSON
MEDIUM: OIL ON BOARD
THE IMPACT OF GLOBAL WARMING ON THE COASTAL ENVIRONMENT.

happy hand

FRANK VIVA

MEDIUM: CHALKS

THE FOLLOWING THREE IMAGES ARE EXPERIMENTAL WORKS. "HAPPY HANDS."

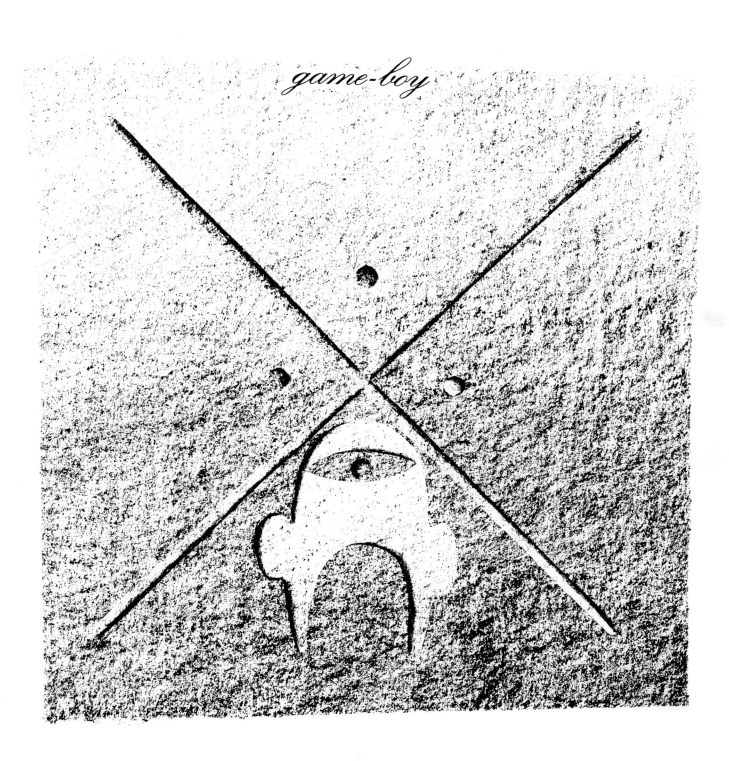

FRANK VIVA

"GAME BOY."

sex object

FRANK VIVA

"SEX OBJECT."

196

RUSSELL O. JONES

MEDIUM: SCRATCH BOARD
A PERSONAL PIECE.

DAVID GOLDIN

MEDIUM: PEN AND INK, WATERCOLOR AND FOUND OBJECTS.
THESE FOUR PIECES ARE PERSONAL WORKS DONE FOR A SOLO SHOW AT THE ILLUSTRATION GALLERY.

DAVID GOLDIN

DAVID GOLDIN

DAVID GOLDIN

ANDREW POWELL

MEDIUM: ACRYLIC, COLLAGE AND PASTEL

THIS ILLUSTRATION WAS INSPIRED BY A CHARACTER FROM FLANNERY O'CONNOR'S STORY
"EVERYTHING THAT RISES MUST CONVERGE," DEPICTING LIFE IN THE SOUTH DURING THE 1960'S.

PEG PASTERNAK

MEDIUM: MIXED MEDIA

"DON JUAN, PART ONE" IS FROM PEG'S "LOVE A GEEK" SERIES.

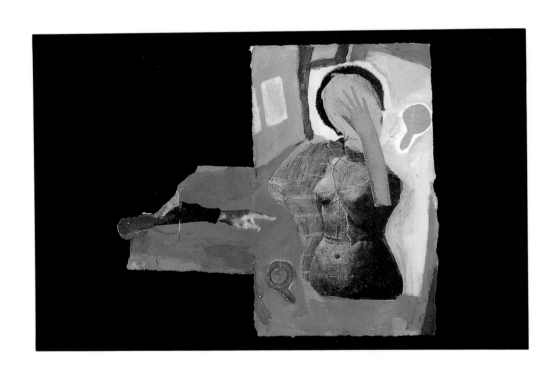

JOELLE NELSON

JOELLE NELSON

MEDIUM: ACRYLIC AND CUT PAPER

''WOMAN THINKING, WITH HER ART ON THE WALL AND THE SKY ABOVE HER.''

MASAKO EBATO

MEDIUM: ARTIST BOOK WITH MIXED MEDIA
"FEBRUARY 13, 1991; VISUAL DIARY, VOL 1."

Masako Ebata

Medium: Oil on wood
''The Bomb Shelter, 1991; Room No. B4–5.''

JOHN COLLIER

ART DIRECTOR: RICHARD SOLOMON

MEDIUM: PASTEL

"THE DOWN SIZING OF AMERICAN BUSINESS" APPEARED IN RICHARD SOLOMON'S 1992 PROMOTION – "FOLIO."

GREG GUTBEZAHL

Medium: Acrylic

"SURFREALISTIC BEACH BLANKET BIRTHDAY" IS THE NAME OF THIS PIECE, USED AS A PARTY INVITATION.

TIM MOORE

MEDIUM: MIXED MEDIA
"WAITING FOR YVES."

Cole Porter writes songs in his sleep.

BARRY BLITT

MEDIUM: PEN AND INK AND WATERCOLOR
"COLE PORTER WRITES SONGS IN HIS SLEEP" WAS CREATED FOR A PERSONAL SKETCHBOOK.

EDMUND GUY

A COLLAGE PORTRAIT OF SPIKE LEE.

EDMUND GUY

A COLLAGE PORTRAIT OF COUNT BASIE.

EDMUND GUY

A collage of American youths hanging out.

JORDIN ISIP

ART DIRECTOR: NOEL CLARO   EDITOR: MARY KAYE SCHILLING
MEDIUM: MIXED MEDIA
THIS ILLUSTRATION FOR A FICTION STORY ENTITLED "CHICAGO" WAS COMMISSIONED BY SASSY MAGAZINE, BUT NEVER PUBLISHED.

LORI DELL

MEDIUM: MIXED MEDIA AND ASSEMBLAGE
A PERSONAL WORK ENTITLED "HOME IS A CASTLE."

MICHAEL MORENKO

MEDIUM: OIL AND ACRYLIC

"SMOKE STACKS," EXECUTED IN 1991 FOR ARTIST'S PORTFOLIO.

KAREN BARBOUR

MEDIUM: OIL ON CANVAS

''FOUR ON BEACH.''

KAREN BARBOUR

MEDIUM: GOUACHE AND INK ON PAPER

"MAN IN FOREST."

KAREN BARBOUR

MEDIUM: INK ON PAPER
''MAN AND BUGS.''

KAREN BARBOUR

MEDIUM: INK

''WALKING MAN.''

GERALD BUSTAMANTE

ART DIRECTOR: DAVID CARSON
MEDIUM: ACRYLIC ON BOARD
A CELEBRATION OF ONENESS WITH NATURE THRU THE JOY OF SURFING,
THIS IMAGE WAS COMMISSIONED BUT NEVER PUBLISHED BY SURFER MAGAZINE.

ERIC DINYER

MEDIUM: MIXED MEDIA AND PHOTOGRAPHY

IRENE ROFHEART

"HAND HOLDING A HOSE ON FLORAL BACKGROUND."

VIVIENNE FLESHER

MEDIUM: PASTEL ON PAPER
A SELF-PROMOTIONAL PIECE.

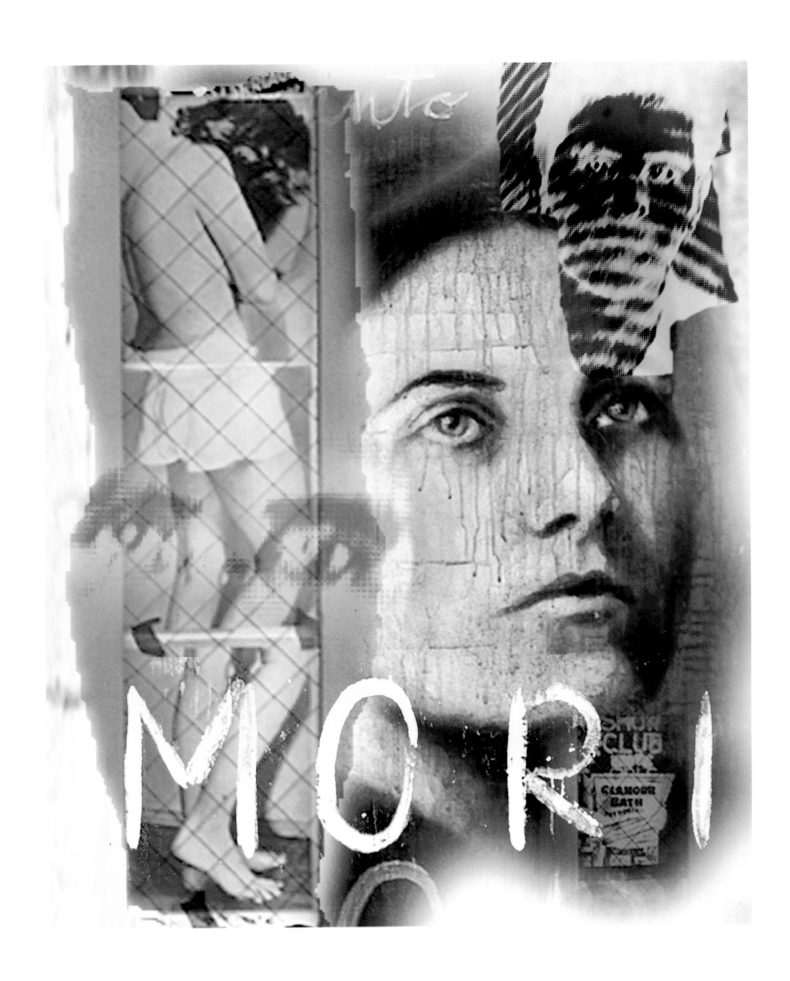

JOSH GOSFIELD

MEDIUM: COMPUTER GENERATED
A PERSONAL PIECE.

JOSH GOSFIELD

MEDIUM: OIL

THE FOLLOWING TWO PIECES WERE COMMISSIONED, BUT NEVER USED FOR BLOOMINGDALE'S SHOPPING BAGS.

JOSH GOSFIELD

PATRICIA LANGUEDOC

MEDIUM: COLLAGE, GOUACHE, GOLD LEAF, AND PEN AND INK.

THIS IMAGE IS ONE OF A PERSONAL SERIES DEALING WITH FEAR, FRUSTRATION AND BELIEFS.

KIM DEMARCO

MEDIUM: WATERCOLOR AND BLACK INK
A PERSONAL WORK.

GARY BASEMAN

MEDIUM: MIXED MEDIA

PERSONAL PIECE ON THEME OF "CHAOS AND EMPTINESS."

GARY BASEMAN

MEDIUM: ACRYLIC
PERSONAL PIECE ON "INSPIRATION."

GARY BASEMAN

MEDIUM: MIXED
UNUSED IMAGE FOR AMERICAN ILLUSTRATION 10 COVER.

JOEL BOWER

MEDIUM: ACRYLIC AND COLORED PENCIL
"WORKING WOMAN" WAS CREATED FOR THE ARTIST'S PORTFOLIO – "BUILDING ON INSPIRATION TOGETHER."

TOM SULLY

MEDIUM: OIL

TRIPTYCH PAINTED IN AN AMERICAN REGIONALIST STYLE DEPICTING A WORKER AND THE LANDSCAPE OF RECESSION.

PHILIPPE LARDY

ART DIRECTOR: EDWARD BOOTH-CLIBBORN
MEDIUM: GOUACHE ON INDIAN PAPER
THIS ILLUSTRATION WAS CREATED FOR THE 1992 AMERICAN ILLUSTRATION CALL FOR ENTRIES POSTER.

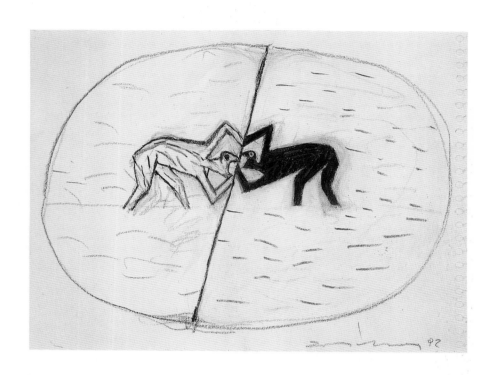

MARIAN C. ZACHAROW

MEDIUM: COLOR PENCIL AND ACRYLIC ON PAPER
"TWO FIGURES IN CIRCLE WITH BOUNDARIES."

ANN FIELD

MEDIUM: ACRYLIC PAINT ON CANVAS

PERSONAL WORK PAINTED FROM LIFE AND IMAGINATION ENTITLED "PASSION."

238

TERI MICCO

MEDIUM: OIL ON CANVAS

''LEAVE-TAKING.''

CAROL D. FABRICATORE

MEDIUM: OIL

THIS IS ONE IN A SERIES OF PAINTINGS DEPICTING STREET-WALKERS IN NEW YORK CITY.

INDEX